Electronic pathways

Adult learning and the
new communication technologies

Electronic pathways

Adult learning and the
new communication technologies

edited by Jane Field

NIACE
THE NATIONAL ORGANISATION
FOR ADULT LEARNING

Published by the National Institute of Adult Continuing Education
(England and Wales)
21 De Montfort Street, Leicester, LE1 7GE
Company registration no. 2603322
Charity registration no. 1002775

First published 1997
©NIACE

CATALOGUING IN PUBLICATION DATA
A CIP record for this title is available from the British Library
ISBN 1 86201 008 0

Typeset by Midlands Book Typesetters
Text design by Virman Man
Cover design by Sue Storey
Printed in Great Britain by Biddles, Guildford and King's Lynn

CONTENTS

Introduction

Introduction

Jane Field

Like it or not, the information society is affecting all of us in our everyday lives. What are the implications for those concerned with adult learning? How can we best exploit modern technologies without diminishing the learning experience? Do adult learners want access to communication technologies? This book argues that there are opportunities in adult education for using the modern communication technologies, that the experience for both adult educators and adult learners can be stimulating and that access to the new technologies can widen opportunities for the future.

In recent years those working in further and higher education (FHE) have experimented with and developed a range of new teaching methods using the opportunities offered by the new technologies. The majority of these developments have been confined to mainstream university or FE teaching. How can relative newcomers make sense of this fast-developing field of practice, and make best use of the opportunities it is creating?

This book offers practitioners guidance, examples of good practice and advice on sources of information and support. Alternative methods for delivering courses, enhanced communication amongst students and tutors and the opportunities of presenting text on-screen are just some of the issues addressed. It will enable the reader to make an informed decision about whether or not to proceed with further exploration of the opportunities presented through telematics – a term increasingly used across Europe to refer to the convergence of computing and communication, leading to the integration of information and telecommunications technologies. Above all, there are arguments presented throughout the book that the use of new technologies can enhance opportunities for adult learning. This is not to say that all traditional classes and methods of teaching and learning should be abandoned – far from it. Rather, the authors believe that telematics widen the scope for adult educators, present solutions to some dilemmas and provide alternatives to the more traditional teaching modes.

Information and communication technologies are moving forward at a tremendous rate. Television advertisements include World Wide Web site addresses, colleagues casually exchange e-mail addresses and friends keep in touch through quick messages across the internet. People 'attend' conferences on a screen via video link, children's book clubs sell CD ROM packages, touch-phone recorded messages infuriate many of us trying to book a seat for the cinema or an aeroplane. Inevitably, communication technologies are increasingly available within the workplace. There is now widespread experience of video and audio conferencing, CD ROM, e-mail, the world wide web, computer conferencing and satellite transmission.

But all too often developments in the new communication technologies have been confined to those working in specialist information technology and telematics spheres. Many books are available on telematics, communication technologies and the impact of multimedia and interactive systems, but most are targeted at the informed technologist or student specialising in this area. Others offer an elegant analytical overview but provide little or no practical advice to the practitioner. Adult educators, community groups and adult learners are generally among those who rarely have access to or an awareness of the opportunities offered by technology, or conversely the problems it may present.

Many of the barriers that once prevented educators and trainers from implementing new technologies are disappearing. A great deal of hardware exists, and the technical infrastructure to facilitate access to the new communication technologies is available within most colleges and universities, and more recently may be found in community outreach centres. Actually using the hardware, sending an e-mail message, contributing to a seminar or discussion via video link, accessing the Internet as a research tool, developing and using multi-media teaching and learning materials, or participating in a computer conference are no longer activities confined to the 'techno-whizzes', but are opportunities available to an increasingly larger number of people.

Adult educators, whether working in FHE institutions, community-based or having responsibility for staff training in the private sector, are amongst those for whom telematics might offer interesting solutions. Yet, ironically, the barrier that does exist in many institutions is that of developing the key resource, people. Little or no staff development is offered at an organisational level. More often than not, those who could practically exploit this technology do not have an understanding of the potential offered.

While some universities are developing modules to enable all undergraduate students to have access to learning about and using new communication technologies, few such opportunities are available to non-specialist adults. Information technology (IT) is a core skill in the 16–19-year-old framework (GNVQs and NVQs); and within the national curriculum pupils in schools have exposure to IT. This immediately points to an awareness and skills deficit amongst older people.

One of the difficulties for the 'techno-phobe', or the majority of us who are not working on a daily basis with leading-edge technologies, is how to find out more. Occasionally journals print an interesting article about the use of new technology; colleagues may be running courses with video-links; and many FHE organisations now have a home page on the Web – but, how to get involved? Many people talk about telematics, sounding knowledgeable and *au fait* with the terminology and the technology but actually the application of telematics in adult learning is still in its infancy.

This book is divided into four sections. The first considers the relationship between telematics and adult learning; this is followed by fourteen case studies. The third section offers checklists developed from the practical experience of those who have exploited communication technologies; the last section gives the NIACE and European Union perspectives and the book concludes with a short glossary. The focus is on the opportunities for teaching adults through new communication technologies, which in itself can be an important way of learning more about the potential of telematics. In the same way, adults who are encouraged to participate in learning activities using telematics will also learn more about communication technologies, will gain experience and skills in using communications technologies and will have some degree of confidence to use them in other situations, whether at work, in leisure activities, further training or education opportunities.

The first five chapters consider modern communication technologies within an adult education framework. The authors all come with some considerable experience of working in adult education, and have themselves addressed the practicalities and benefits to the learner of accessing modern communication technologies.

Telematics in education and training provides an introductory overview. It looks at the range of technologies available, the needs of adult learners and how telematics might be used by adult educators. Winders claims that 'the use of telematics adds a third dimension to the dichotomy between face-to-face and distance learning'.

From a Canadian perspective Martin Buck's chapter *The global demands for change* looks at the push for and response to the use of new communication technologies in education and training. He cites examples of strategies for the coming of the information age from across the world. This chapter explains some of the terms and concepts that are likely to be common-place in the future and briefly considers the potential for the effective use of telematics in the context of adult learning.

Jill Mannion Brunt's chapter *Can you put your arm around a student on the internet?* expands on ideas from her paper initially published in *Adults Learning* (January 1996). She argues emphatically that the needs of adult learners, and a student-centred approach, should not be forsaken in the development of new technology-based teaching and learning materials. 'Taking control of their own learning is something which comes with experience, success and confidence'.

Chapter Four starts with John Field's claim that 'new communications technologies are changing the educational landscape'. *The adult learner as listener, viewer and cybersurfer* explores the use of new technologies in entertainment and to support learning; and the implications for adult educators. Field offers a number of issues that might be addressed by those seeking to develop a strategy for the use of telematics in education.

In the final chapter in this section, *Teaching and learning with the new technologies,* Paul Helm reflects on the added value, or otherwise, that new technology has to offer. Calling on his own and others' experiences, he evaluates the findings from interviews with students who have participated in courses using new technologies, and considers the advantages and disadvantages that they identify. Buck and Field, in earlier chapters, give some thought to what the future holds; Helm's view of the future use of new technologies in education is perhaps the most radical. It cannot be denied that 'the single most powerful determinant of the successful use of new technologies in education will be the creativity of individual teachers and the strength of their desire to improve their courses'.

The case studies provide fourteen examples of how the contributors have experimented with, explored and delivered teaching and learning programmes using communication technologies. They outline the practicalities of setting up the necessary hardware in centres, studios and students' homes. The design and use of teaching and learning materials using, for example, CD-ROM or the World Wide Web, is examined. New and different ways by which students communicate with each other and their tutors, including e-mail, video links and computer conferencing, are described. Two examples of using telematics applications for staff development within universities are included.

Opportunities for distance learning, with accessible, interactive tutor support and group participation represents a real challenge for adult educators today. Oh no, not another challenge! There are numerous new and exciting and downright tedious challenges being posed or imposed on adult education and learning today, and why should the challenge of communication technologies be any more than a passing phase? To start, it offers mechanisms for distance and open learning through a range of options, which used together make the term 'multi-media' come to life. There is a real breakthrough in delivering courses to individuals and groups who previously have been restricted access for various reasons. Video conferencing breaks down the barriers imposed by distance, time and travel costs, so that it is possible to have a meeting of the community in Enniskillen, County Fermanagh (Northern Ireland) with representatives from the community in Poplar Bluff, Missouri (USA) or an input from a member of the European Parliament to an academic conference, with the opportunity for questions and answers after the presentation. Access to specialists and experts, world-wide, will open up intercultural communication and learning. Telematics is breaking down the barriers between working and learning, and those who have an understanding of communication technologies may soon be better placed in both environments.

While the contributors have all experienced some level of success, the case studies introduce a note of realism and caution, and address some of the practical problems. Many of the projects described have only recently started, others are more mature; but in every case the authors have thoughts about possible future developments, which they share with the reader. The case studies make exciting reading, and it is useful to remind ourselves that less than a decade ago many of these developments would have been unthinkable.

Section Three provides three checklists, where the experience of others can be used to the benefit of those entering the field. Examples of good practice, pitfalls to avoid (or be aware of) and opportunities are provided in a simple checklist format.

In Section Four Stephen McNair, Associate Director for Research and Development at the National Institute of Adult Continuing Education (NIACE), describes the priorities identified by NIACE in their recently-developed strategy for the use of telematics in adult learning. John Field gives an overview of the European Union's (EU) approach to telematics and 'the information society' and describes the funding programmes that support developments in the use of telematics in education and training. This includes brief descriptions of some of the projects that have received funding under the EU's programmes for research, education and vocational training.

With the advent of information technology a new vocabulary emerged. Not surprisingly, this has developed further with telematics users. Some of the most commonly used terms, phrases and acronyms are given in the glossary at the end of the book.

The new communication technologies certainly blur the boundaries to the ways in which we previously looked at things. For example the telephone, television and personal computers are all accepted as standard forms of communication. Through the exploitation of new technologies it is possible to have all these methods of communication connected through the same socket, and to make use of all three at the same time. A further fuzzy issue, and one that seems to be giving difficulty to some, is that employers, the leisure industry and education could all be using the same technologies (eg tele-workers, home shopping and open learning courses). To adult educators this very 'fuzziness' could further support the view that adult learners should be exposed to the new communication technologies.

This book aims to offer a general understanding of some of the potential of the new technologies for anyone working in the field of adult education and training. It is designed to be a handbook, with readers selecting areas in which they have an interest, or about which they want to know more. None of the authors assumes a comprehensive knowledge of the new technologies – quite the reverse. Each contribution is deliberately meant to demystify the new technologies, to acknowledge their limitations, and to open up ways of exploiting the real potential that they offer.

Section One

Chapter One

The use of telematics in education and training

Ray Winders

Television and video recording are a part of most homes in Europe. In education and training the use of this medium is no more challenging than using a book. The other basis of telematics, the use of computers, is different. There are relatively few computers in homes but most school classrooms contain several 'desktops'. Adult learners are therefore familiar with television as a broadcast or recorded medium but less familiar with computers. This will change gradually as the schoolchildren of the 1990s move into adult education. In this chapter the use of telematics in education and training is examined, with particular emphasis on the needs of adult learners both now and in the next decade.

There are many models of learning, most involving a learning cycle. For the purpose of this chapter we can use a basic model, then look at what can be offered by the technologies at our disposal now and in the near future, and then finally bring the two together to examine how telematics can contribute to each stage of the cycle.

Educational cycle

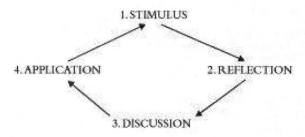

Fig 1. Educational cycle

This simplified diagram indicates four stages in learning. The cycle continues after stage four as a new cycle, and may be viewed as a spiral with each circuit reaching a higher level! Alternatively each circle may be regarded as a stitch in a tapestry which when completed creates an overview of the subject.

Stimulus The learner must *want* to learn. For adults there are two separate stimuli. First is interest and inspiration. Adults who spend their evenings at their own expense in anything from 'Painting in Acrylics' to 'Fundamentals of Twentieth Century

Philosophy' are there because they want to be there. In contrast adults may be driven by a need to earn a living or to cope with a crisis or to remedy a deficiency which they see in their lifestyle. Over the last century there have been many debates over the division between education and training; for adults perhaps the division is exemplified above. The challenge in both education and training is to provide a stimulus which will first attract the learner to begin the course and then to continue. Can telematics provide this stimulus at a distance? Jill Mannion Brunt, John Field and Paul Helm consider the needs of adult learners and what telematics might offer in the following chapters.

Reflection   The effective stimulus session should send the learner away with a range of information and ideas. Most adult classes occur at intervals and the learner is able to concentrate on one topic. There is therefore a period in which the student can classify the information and ideas and compare them with previous knowledge and experience.

Discussion   This is an important stage in both clarification and development. Articulating new ideas and comparing these with ideas expressed by colleagues confirms what has been achieved and exposes gaps and misconceptions. If the group is unable to agree then a further 'stimulus' session may be required. Can videoconferencing and similar electronic meetings support this discussion effectively?

Application   At this stage the new learning is tested in real life. The theory of the self-assertiveness course must bear fruit in your next encounter with a hostile driver. World Wide Web training must be applied by searching for information of value to the individual when it is actually required.

Technologies

The telematics technologies available to us can, for convenience, be divided into three groups, though as technologies converge the distinctions are becoming more blurred.

- Presentation media – television, slides, data-projection.
- Computers – screens of data, graphics and multi-media.
- Communication media – computer conferencing, video-conferencing, satellite distribution of programmes and data, internet.

It is the third of these, the communication media, which may make the most fundamental change in adult education. Presentation media and desktop computers improve the quality and enhancement of the information available to us. Communication technologies, particularly those which encourage interaction, take us a step forward to a stage at which information and ideas are exchanged, but participants do not have to travel. Video-conferencing gives the village hall the same status as the city centre college.

Presentation media   The uses of television and 35mm slides to illustrate sessions and to stimulate discussion are familiar to all. A new generation of presentation devices is now beginning, as television cameras become smaller and cheaper, and as computer displays can be projected. Colour TV cameras costing less than £200 can now be used to enlarge pictures, diagrams and specimens to a television screen or to a larger audience, through a video projector. They can be purchased mounted on a stand with push button controls. Computer outputs can be displayed to an audience by two methods. The first is a shallow box or 'tablet' which sits on the glass of an overhead projector. The computer is connected to the tablet for a full colour presentation of what is on the computer screen, including any movements of the cursor and resultant screen movements. The second device is a separate projector, which provides large screen images direct from a computer, or from a video player. The tablet has the advantage of easy portability, particularly if used with a lap-top computer. Video projectors are heavier but still no larger than a briefcase, and have the advantage of brighter output. The travelling tutor can, using those devices, both carry large quantities of stored information and display screens effectively to the audience.

Computers   The contribution of computers in adult education is wide. At the most basic level, word processing enables students to prepare and share documents of good quality with approved spelling. The use of spreadsheets and graphics packages allows the tutor and the student to present information quickly and clearly, and to update the screen to match the rapid changes in current society.

The newer generation of multi-media computers enhances presentation but creates new dimensions. The storage capacity of CD ROM, particularly of series of images, enables the individual to interact with quality sources. A building or a crystal can be rotated and viewed from any angle. Photographs, graphics, sounds and moving images can be combined to create the 'ideal' sequence, or the powerful stimulus culminating in virtual reality. In education and training the power of the multi-media computer can be used to offer alternative learning pathways, often in an attractive visual package. It is possible to view a room containing various resources and then to select a bookshelf from the room which leads into a selection of documents. If video is preferred 'click' on the TV set; if French language is preferred click on the Eiffel Tower icon. It is also possible to view a building or an art gallery by selecting various 'doors' to create your own pathway. For more structured learning and training 'adaptive' programmes are appearing. Information is presented which requires a response from the learner. After a sequence of responses, the learning style of the student is assessed and the following screens are then presented in the most effective sequence for the individual learner. As the working of the brain is better understood, the quality of these 'neural networks' will be enhanced. The varied experiences and needs of the adult learner will be utilised and met. This, together with the rapid improvements in the digitisation and compression of information, could provide the ideal personal tutor in a gift wrapped box! The case study *Text, theory, event* (Lisa McRory) addresses some of the issues involved when using CD ROM as a learning resource.

Communication media   Transmission of sound and visuals to distant locations becomes easier as technologies develop. We are currently at the point where digitisation of sound and vision is common in stand-alone devices, such as stereo systems, but is only just beginning to have an impact in business in terms of digital telephones and in particular digitised video transmission. Digitisation and compression of both audio and video signals will make possible distance delivery of education and training at progressively lower cost. This is therefore a vitally important time for all in education to use and evaluate these media as they appear, and ensure that each development takes its place as part of a progressive strategy, rather than as a series of reactions to the latest wonder of electronics. Some of the systems available to us at present are identified next, with an emphasis on their *use* and potential.

Available systems

Telephone and audio conferencing   The telephone is already widely used for one-to-one tutorials in distance education, and more fundamentally for communication between students. The provision of a telephone bridge allows more than two telephones to be connected, to provide a group conversation. Access to the bridge is rented by the hour, so no special equipment is required to participate, though the use of a hands-free phone facilitates note-taking and is more comfortable in a long discussion. Since the participants have no visual communication, there is no feedback from expression or body language. Careful chairing is necessary to ensure that each participant contributes and that all are clear on the outcomes. Support notes circulated beforehand are useful, but must have clear headings so that a particular section can be found by each individual. Experience suggests that audioconferencing is most effective as a support to face-to-face meetings, or as a periodic tutorial in support of a traditional paper-based course. The first three case studies offer different angles on the use of videoconferencing. They show how studios have been set up (Smith) and how videoconferencing has been used with adult learners (Robinson) and with communities through outreach centres (Leal).

Computer conferencing   Connecting a computer to a traditional analogue telephone line requires a 'modem' to convert the digital computer data to analogue. Many educational organisations operate their own computer networks to which the distant student can be connected using a modem. There are three current applications which are important for adult education and training.

● Access to information
  There are three case studies on the World Wide Web. Two are student-based examples: Porter and Childs (UK) and Buck (Canada); and one for staff development, Rhen (Australia). The Internet provides almost unlimited information ranging from electronic encyclopaedias to availability of seats on today's Concorde to New York. In the UK, the Joint Academic Network JANET, and her successor SUPERJANET, allows searchers access to a more structured environment including access to international journals. Though the cost of a modem and the monthly access charge are relatively low, telephone costs can mount rapidly for the home student. The development of local access points at local telephone rates will be an important step forward, particularly for rural learners.

● Live conferencing
  Dialogue using computers is possible by electronic mail. It is cheaper than speech and particularly useful to remote areas such as Eastern Europe, where an e-mail can find a space in telephone links which do not have enough speech capacity. Exchanging screens of information is useful in support of telephone conferencing described above. Betty Walsh describes the experience of using e-mail for communication between students located at two university campuses in Australia.

● Asynchronous conferencing
  Most computer conferencing is done by leaving a message for later reply. This

gives the respondent a chance to think about the answer and collect information if required. A computer conference can be continued between a group to create a longer-term dialogue. A research project at Exeter University is evaluating a link between a UK local network and a parallel network in Virginia USA, for the exchange of experiences between students in teacher training (Davis 1992). A useful activity is for the tutor to set a question to which each student replies, thus building up a visible dialogue (all students can see the answers on their own screens). This can then be summarised by the tutor or used as the basis for a telephone conference.

Case studies from Sankey and Dibble; and Lewis, Goulde and Ryan show the benefits and problems experienced when using computer conferencing as a method of communication between course participants.

Digital networks   The introduction of digital telephone networks has supported faster transmission of voice and data including, at present, limited motion video. ISDN (Integrated Services Digital Network) videoconferencing is beginning to have a place in distance education. Two digital lines are used with a total capacity of 128 Kbits/sec. A typical low-cost system adds a card and software to an existing computer. A small camera sits on top of the computer, and a digital telephone is provided. Using this, it is possible to connect together a group to share screens of information, and make corrections or emphasise specific points on all screens simultaneously. The camera sends an image of the persons at the computer. Movement at present is jerky since the system samples the changes rather than sending a continuous image as in broadcast television. The University of Ulster uses videoconferencing to link remote classrooms (Abbott et al 1994) and found that this has been particularly useful in supporting groups of students working together at each location. Alan Robinson's case study describes this experience in some detail, considering the benefits of videoconferencing for adult educators.

Satellite transmission   At present ISDN videoconferencing will not carry full motion video and is best suited to linking a limited number of centres. The use of satellite transmission supports broadcast-standard transmission to an unlimited number of sites. A typical satellite 'footprint' would cover the whole of Europe. At the University of Plymouth a series of projects supported by the European Space Agency has used satellite transmission of live programmes in combination with telephone and computer conferencing, to enable students at a distance to question the studio experts. Recently, the provision of an ISDN videoconference link in studio has enabled questioners to appear in the programme, but more importantly to enable experts at a distance to make a contribution direct from their company or university. A problem has been the cost of renting time on commercial satellites. This is only viable with a large number of students though several universities in the USA offer courses by satellite. The next series of programmes will use new technologies for the digitisation and compression of the signal to 2.5 Mbite. This is indistinguishable to the viewer, but reduces the cost of satellite rental to 20 per cent. Adrian Vranch, later in this book, provides a case study of a satellite-delivered programme. Satellite transmission supported by videoconferencing can provide a 'world-class' presentation, irrespective of the location of the learner. Unlike computer networks described above, once the satellite-receiving equipment has been purchased there are no line rental charges. For the provider there are no extra costs to reach extra sites, and there is no limit imposed by the existence of cables. This is particularly important for rural areas where cable delivery is often not economic.

Cable systems   In city areas of the UK cable television is available on rental. At present only 20 per cent of homes in which cable is available use the service. There are several channels available on the network some of which are unused. In the USA some companies have made a channel available for community education and information. In Los Angeles, a community channel is devoted to ethnic groups. They produce their own very low cost programmes, normally in their own language. There is considerable potential for the use of cable in the delivery of adult education to the home in urban areas. This is particularly appropriate for the elderly, the disabled and those who are reluctant to leave their homes in the evening. Since in the UK cable franchises are relatively local, the development of adult education programmes would require a joint initiative between providers and cable companies. Costs of delivery could be very low per capita.

Integration

How do the technologies outlined above relate to the learning cycle? Each stage will be considered in turn.

Stimulus   Traditionally stimulus has been provided either by face-to-face presentations or by structured packages. Both modes have been enhanced by telematics. The tutor has regularly used slides and video to enhance presentations: now the facility to project direct from the computer provides enhanced graphics and access to real spreadsheets or word processing screens. If the computer can be linked to the Internet then the group can share worldwide access.

Distance learning packages still rely on the printed word, but many now contain computer disks, some of which provide opportunities for participation. The addition of CD ROM provides quality images which transform distance learning in subjects such as Art and Design and Biology. Distance learning packages can be expensive to produce and can take time in preparation, which often involves an expert team. This mode is most appropriate for large student populations as in the Open University, and in subjects where information is relatively static.

The use of telematics adds a third dimension to the dichotomy between face-to-face and distance learning. This could be termed *face-to-face at a distance*. The use of videoconferencing and satellite delivery allows the expert to address groups at a distance. The audience can ask questions by telephone, e-mail or videoconference.

A tutor can make a presentation to a class who are in the room, but at the same time be seen and questioned by remote groups on a videoconference link. They can also present their views or findings to the other groups. Satellite delivery from a television studio enhances the presentation, since video can be used and presentation assisted by vision mixing. 'Face-to-face at a distance' has the advantage of interaction and immediacy found in a tutorial but, when well organised and illustrated, has some of the characteristics of a learning package. The final case study looks at some of the ways that University of Bradford Management Centre has used telematics 'to take the Distance out of Distance Learning'.

Reflection   Reflection and internalisation is individual. There is less that can be offered by telematics at this stage. Some students do however find that the logic and links provided by a computer or, alternatively, the capacity to browse widely in search of new ideas or linkages is beneficial.

Discussion   It is at this stage that telematics are of the most immediate benefit. As described above, groups or individuals can communicate at a distance using a range of technologies. The individual isolated by location can join in an audioconference. The individual isolated by shift patterns or personal time constraints can join in an asynchronous computer conference at 2am. The use of telematics to support small groups of learners is particularly important. Stimulus sessions can be followed by structured group activities. The group can then feed back by videoconference to share experience with other members of the distributed class.

Application   Again this is normally an individual activity. Using computers to enhance presentation and to provide information and search facilities will enhance the outcome in an essay or report. It could be argued that use of telematics in learning helps the individual to cope with technology in the workplace and, not insignificantly, to keep up with the children.

Evaluation

Stephen Ehrmann (1995) looked at the use and potential use of telematics in post-secondary education in the USA. He identified a 'triple challenge' to successful implementation:

- The need to extend access to courses and to retain those who enrol.
- The need to maintain and improve quality of learning.
- The need to control costs.

He examined the use of technologies in a number of American university programmes. He found key examples of success when some of the following were present:

- Use of familiar technologies rather than systems specifically designed for education.
- Stimulus sessions delivered by first class experts.
- Access using asynchronous networks.
- Networking and co-operation between providers.
- 100 per cent access.

He found that the two advantages most often cited by students were:

- Savings in time – travel was minimised and computer networks provide information at the desk as needed.
- Access to high quality sources particularly when these were used for group activity.

We have, in this chapter, looked at the advantages for access provided by telematics either to a local centre or direct to home. We have also looked at the potential for enhancing quality. The third factor listed by Ehrmann is cost.

The costs of equipment and rental are to some extent balanced by costs of travel and opportunity to work more effectively. At present, most telematics courses are provided by existing institutions in addition to normal classes. Enrolment of extra students in distant videoconference classrooms may be balanced by enrolment fees. If, however, telematics became more prevalent, the enormous investment in buildings and maintenance, which is a major cost of education provision, would be reduced. If students can access library information from home or from a community centre, central library provision can be drastically reduced. Ehrmann states that the entire telematics network in Maine costs less to install and support than building and running one secondary school.

Telematics can provide an enhancement to presentation and interaction. Both may influence adult education in the next decades. In cities, access to a community cable channel could bring adult education to a number of new audiences, and provide viable access for minorities both in ethnicity and special interest. In rural areas the use of telematics links to bring together scattered students for live sessions again challenges existing notions of viability. Two cases on the rural community (Sue Challis – Shropshire; and McGinley and O'Dubhchair – Co. Fermanagh, N. Ireland) show the use of broadcasting by educational networks to bring in a new dimension of delivery of world class, up-to-the minute teaching sessions, directly to any rural community. A further step towards the global village. The RATIO project just being launched in south west England will provide a testbed in using the full range of telematics to reach 40 rural centres.

References

Abbott, L., Dallat, J., Livingston, R., Robinson, A. (1994) 'The Application of Videoconferencing to the Advancement of Independent Group Learning for Professional Development', *Education and Training Technology International*, vol. 31, no. 2, pp 85–92.

Davis, N. (1992) 'Case Study : A Future for Electronic Communications in Education', *Education and Training Technology International*, vol. 29, no. 4, pp 332–335.

Ehrmann, S. C. (1995) 'Flashlight', *Change*, vol. XXVII, no. 2, pp 20–27.

Chapter Two

The global demands for change

Martin Buck

In the last decades of the second millennium the world has experienced significant transformation. Few sectors of human society have remained unscathed by the movement from a territorial, industrial order to a global information community. With the corresponding increase in world-wide competition, private and public sector institutions have had to resort to greater automation to increase production and cut the largest expense item, employee wages.

A Canadian example will serve to illustrate the effects of the information age on blue collar workers. Just north of the University of Victoria in British Columbia is the town of Chemainus. For most of this century Chemainus has been a lumber mill town. In the early 1980s the mill, which employed over 600 workers, was closed. When a new, more highly automated mill opened a year later, just over a hundred workers were required to produce the same amount of lumber. Few of those hired for the new mill were original employees. The new workers required skills in team building and information technology. These skills, while not called for in the old mill, were absolutely critical to productivity in the new one. The major employment in the town is now in the tourism industry that sprang up around the murals the town put up to celebrate its logging industry past.

Blue collar workers are not the only ones experiencing the discomfort associated with change; more recently middle managers have experienced similar pressures. Traditionally this sector has been charged with managing the information flow to executive decision makers. However, today's electronic information technology allows company operating officers direct, personal access to essential data. In Victoria, the Bank of Montreal 'has fired up to 24 employees who the bank said couldn't keep up with the changing banking industry' (Helm, 1995: September 12, B3). Displaced white collar workers must also find other employment. Typically this new employment is in some form of small business which, as the engine of the new economy, is providing the majority of new jobs (*Times-Colonist*, 1994: B11). These shifts in employment and related job security were confirmed by Canada's Minister of Human Resources, Lloyd Axworthy. Two decades ago a student could complete university and step into a job that promised job security. Now, according to Axworthy (1995), today's graduates have far more difficulty. Even professionals with job security such as lawyers, doctors and teachers are faced with knowledge explosion problems brought about by technology. The American Society for Training and Development estimates that by the end of this decade, 75 per cent of the workforce will need retraining (Twigg, 1994). Adult Basic Education (ABE) upgrading programs are experiencing the effects of this transformation. Adults, many ill-equipped to be the lifelong learners that today's economy demands, are returning to school in increasing numbers. In most cases these students come with an educational background that has not prepared them to be the lifelong learners the information age demands.

The modern education system for the masses is a relatively recent innovation, the origin of which can be traced to the late nineteenth and early twentieth centuries. Today's schooling system is a product of the industrial revolution. In the previous agrarian age most learners received whatever education they needed in the home or workplace. Fathers passed on their skills to their sons, mothers to their daughters. Those who desired a more formal education either paid for a tutor or joined the church. With the industrial age came factories and, by necessity, the public school system. Fathers first, and then mothers, began working outside the home often in a highly structured and specialised environment. The family unit gave way in importance to the factory unit, complete with a supervising foreman. What was to be done with the children?

Western world societies developed the factory model of schooling based on the division of labour model that made industrialisation so efficient and successful. Each teacher, like a factory foreman, was responsible for supervising a group of students. Just as in the industrial age factory, there were bells, buzzers and clocks to tell the student-workers when to begin and end their day. Again, just as in the factory model, obedience to the foreman was critical. Thanks to the melding of citizens schooled in this industrial age manner with industrial age technology, western society prospered. Thus, for as long as the world remained in the industrial age, the factory model served society well. Much of this system remains in place in today's schools. However, with the advent of the information age, increasing criticisms of the factory model of schooling began to be heard.

Current context of the problem

For over two decades educational critics have commented on the problem of schooling. Illich (1971, 1973), Postman (1973), Goodlad (1983), Papert (1988) and Perelman (1993) are just a few of the critics of modern day schooling. They that argue the traditional schooling model is an ineffective, expensive and perhaps even detrimental way of educating today's youth. In 1983, Goodlad presented a number of concerns based on the data from his comprehensive survey of American schooling. He spoke about the difficulty of change and stated that data from his survey suggested 'a formidable agenda'. He was led to some pessimism by the 'great irony . . . of [t]hose who still live in the past confidently set[ting] the norms for educating those who will live in the future (19)'.

> . . . most public school administrators judge teachers on their ability to manage students, comply with directives, and avoid major discipline problems. Whether one's students learn anything or feel good is not relevant. Some students are expected to fail, and most are expected to be bored (Kohl, 30).

According to other critics Kohl's pessimism was neither misplaced nor misguided. Throughout this decade, expressions of concern have continued.

Higher education is also experiencing calls for change. Perelman (1993) in *School's out* criticises the conventional approaches of both public schooling and higher education when he says,

The key to working and prospering in the unfolding new economy of the knowledge age is not education but entrepreneurship. Entrepreneurs need to be prolific learners, but their kind of high-profit learning comes from doing, not from attending classes.

Others, while taking a less radical view, agree that higher education is being confounded by information age paradigm shifts. Carol Twigg is vice president of Educom, a Washington DC-based consortium of colleges and universities seeking to transform education through the use of information technology. She notes that with over 14 million (American) college students, higher education has become a mass phenomenon that '. . . alone simply cannot serve the needs of today's students: it is too restrictive, it is too expensive, and it is often inappropriate' (Twigg, 1994). In the June 1994 issue of *Educational Technology* Professors Kemp and McBeath gather further comments on the need for change in higher education. They quote Derek Bok, president of Harvard University.

The fact is that colleges work hard to provide new facilities, activities and services, but devote remarkably little time to deliberate efforts aimed at improving student learning.

Ernest Boyer, head of The Carnegie Foundation for the Advancement of Teaching maintains,

. . . many of the nation's colleges are more successful in credentialing than in providing a quality education for their students. It is not that the failure of the undergraduate college is too large, but that the institutional expectations often are too small.

Daniel Seymour, former professor and administrator and now President of Qsystems, a quality-management consulting firm, claims,

We are kidding ourselves if we believe that educating people for the year 2000 is essentially the same as educating them for the year 1975. Everything has changed – technology, lifestyles, cultures. Our educational institutions must change as well.

The problems brought about by information age paradigm shifts are global. Peter T. Knight (December 1995), Chief of the World Bank's Electronic Media Center, in a paper presented at the AFRISTECH'95 Symposium on Information Superhighways: What Strategy for Africa? writes,

*The telematics revolution, which has been reducing the cost of processing, storing, and transmitting information on the order of 50 per cent every 18 months for the past 40 years . . . is causing what **The Economist** in its recent special study called 'the death of distance.' It is profoundly affecting the way we live, learn, produce, and consume. In an increasingly knowledge-based economy, the impact on the speed and nature of learning is particularly significant, and lies at the very heart of this revolution.*

Those actively involved in research in adult education, like Patricia Cross (1986), also recognise that transformations brought about by new technologies have brought major social and political changes to the workforce.

The explosion of knowledge means that almost all professionals are self-directed learners; but most are also spending increasing amounts of time in a wide variety of organised learning activities.

If technological changes and the resulting knowledge explosion have made lifelong learning necessary, they also offer a means to help educational institutions meet these needs.

In March 1995 the British Columbia Student Outcomes Steering Committee completed the James report on the effectiveness of Adult Basic Education programmes in provincial colleges. One of the major findings of the study was the identification of the adult student's '. . . need for more flexible course scheduling and delivery. Adult Basic Education (ABE) Student Outcomes Steering Committee, March, 1995'. Many ABE programmes offer flexibility through continuous intake, individualised instruction and year-round programming. However, classroom instruction continues to be just that, instruction offered in a classroom at set times and set locations. The need for greater flexibility is readily recognised by most adult educators. Many adult learners come to ABE programs with a set of challenges that few high school youth graduates face. More and more adult students are supporting single-parent families. Others are dealing with addiction issues. Increasingly low self-esteem due to unemployment and under-employment is also an issue. The list of barriers to education faced by mature learners is long. The James report discovered that due to these obstacles the majority of ABE learners take at least five years to complete their upgrading programme.

The demands for flexibility in programming come at a time when governments are cutting funds to post-secondary education. Thus a major goal of a knowledge age curriculum is to utilise appropriate technologies and systems to allow faculty and staff to effectively increase services to students. The business world has already demonstrated how the application of information technology can increase effectiveness. The appropriate use of these same technologies in the service of students may well provide similar gains in efficiency.

A look to the future – some terms and concepts

The machine as cognition enhancer

Christopher Dede (1989) discusses how evolving information technologies are transforming the nature of work and in turn can positively affect the design and content of the school curriculum. We are beginning to experience 'cognition enhancers' that combine 'complimentary strengths of a person and an information technology' (23). One category of a cognition enhancer is the empowering environment in which the machine handles the routine mechanics of a task, while the person is immersed in its higher-order meanings. The following example will serve to illustrate the point. A woman wanted to play the guitar, but found the task of tuning a guitar beyond her. She bought an electronic tuner which provided visual feedback when the guitar was properly tuned. She was soon playing regularly in a Sunday church service. The word processor with spelling and grammar checker, thesaurus and graphics capabilities provides other good examples. Adult learners should have access to these tools.

Hypermedia and the Internet

Another cognition enhancer, which provides educators with 'a framework for creating an interconnected, web-like representation of symbols (text, graphics, images, software codes). . .' (Dede, 24) is called hypermedia. To understand this software programme, imagine a series of transparent cards. Attached to each of these cards is a button. Each of these buttons can activate an educational resource or information provider. This could be a video segment, a textbook or an encyclopedia. Increasingly it could also be a telecommunications connection to such computer networked resources as electronically stored texts, graphics, sound and video as well as other students and teachers. The user would then be linked to any information, person or place desired. 'Hypermedia is the scholar's and the scientist's dream' (Lemke, 1993). The emerging hypermedia capabilities of networked computers are already dramatically altering learning paradigms. The world's largest computer network, connecting educational, government and commercial institutions in over 35 countries, is called the Internet.

What is the Internet? According to the winning entry in a BBC competition to describe the Internet,

> *The Net is possibly the largest store of information on this planet. Everybody can be part of it; it is one of the few places where race, creed, colour, gender, sexual preference do not prejudice people against others. All this through the magic of modern technology. Communication is the key. People talking to people. The Net isn't computers. That's just the way we access it. The Net is people helping each other in a worldwide community. (Simon Cooke, physics student, quoted in the World Wide Web document titled* Highways for Learning *published in paper and on the Net at http://ncet.csv.warwick.ac.uk/www/randd/highways)*

The Internet is composed of over 30,000 smaller computer networks operated by universities, colleges, research centres, government agencies, non-profit and commercial organisations connecting 30 million people. It is estimated there could be 125 million users world-wide within two years. Net connections range in price from free, for many faculty members and students, to less than two dollars an hour for a connection to a commercial Internet provider site in the world. Once a personal computer has been connected to the Internet any information stored at virtually any site anywhere in the world is available free of additional charge.

> *What was once the playground of an academic, American male, computing elite, now offers something for everyone. Each person sees it differently: for one it may be the largest library on the planet to browse and contribute materials to; for another the fastest and most reliable postal service in the world; for still others it is a way to meet friends, to discuss politics and music, to share views and to exchange help and support. (*Highways for Learning, *1995: 3)*

The hypermedia curriculum development opportunities available on the Net will only grow as more and more educators get connected. In British Columbia the Ministry of Education, Skills, and Training has committed to link every school, college, institute and university in the province to this resource.

> *Libraries and computer centres will integrate their functions. There will be seamless connections of local-area networks and wide-area ones, so that we will as readily use*

this medium to share instructional materials with our students (as they will share their projects with us) as to share professional work with our colleagues. And this in turn will revolutionize the paradigm of education and learning itself . . . (Lemke, 1993)

Cognition enhancers which are continuing to enter the global marketplace, irrevocably altering the workplace, are also having a profound impact on instructional practice, as well as curriculum content and design. Facilitated by telematics, Dede claims the emergence of the following:

- a new definition of human intelligence; a partnership between human strengths and the computer's cognition enhancing capabilities,
- a greater emphasis on collaborative learning as combined computer and telecommunications technologies allows individuals and communities in a variety of places and circumstances to interact,
- improved methods of assessing individual learning needs,
- lifelong 'learning-while-doing', thanks to these same telecomputing networking capabilities,
- a curricular shift from presenting data to evaluating and synthesising ideas, and
- a focus on solving real-world problems using concepts and skills from multiple subject areas. (Dede, 1989: 25–26)

Informatics

Another name for the innovations supporting the objectives outlined above is 'informatics – computers linked to electronic communication systems' (Knappler, 1988: 92). An informatics curriculum can provide 'fundamental skills for the new hypermedia literacy' (Lemke, 1993). These skills include database exploration, information search and retrieval and other user skills, as well as authoring skills. With the world's information base becoming broader and deeper at an exponential rate, database exploration will be a critical skill in an environment where '. . . students will frequently be expected to change from one area of work to another and quickly 'catch up' with its problems and issues'. Lemke). Beyond awareness of the wealth of information available on the Internet are the electronic/Internet skills necessary to locate and retrieve a specific bit of information. Once information is retrieved the learner will need hypermedia navigation skills. Just as the printing press brought about the demand for a new range of skills, so too will hypermedia.

Convergence

Convergence is one of the factors driving these changes. All of the world's information sources are being converted into, and converging to, one digital format. This digitised information can then be delivered via an interconnected series of computer networks called the Internet. These information sources include the traditional media of print, graphics, audio, video and film. Every medium of instruction used in the classroom can now be delivered beyond the four walls of the physical classroom through network tools like e-mail and the World Wide Web. Every information source known to humans can be expressed in a digital form stored on computers connected through this world wide network. Once put into a digital format, information stored on the Net can be readily transmitted at the speed of light through a rapidly growing number of global connections.

The World Wide Web

The World Wide Web (Web) has become the easiest and most effective way to interact with information on the Internet. Not only is it possible to receive text electronically, like this document, but a properly equipped multimedia personal computer can receive graphics, video, audio and indeed any information in binary form. By the year 2000, according to a keynote speaker at the University of British Columbia's WRITE conference, 95 per cent of the world's information will be digitised. The World Wide Web is rapidly becoming the Internet's principal means of electronically publishing and distributing this information.

> *Every ten weeks the number of computers providing information on the World Wide Web doubles. You can use the Web to visit museums, art galleries, libraries and exhibitions, even the White House and soon concerts, all for the cost of a local phone call. You can access the Library of Congress, science resources, journals, book reviews, business statistics, geological survey maps, United Nations papers, music, French language press reviews, software archives, sport databases, magazine archives. You can obtain weather details for most of the globe, images of outerspace; the bible is there, all the novels of Mark Twain, the plays of Shakespeare, the scripts of Blackadder. You can drop in on peoples' lives and homes. The pictures, text data, video and audio files can be copied and saved for your own use (subject to copyright.)*
> (Highways for Learning, 1995, 4)

Educators are beginning to see the potential in the Web for delivering instructional modules to learners in a time and space independent manner (Ministry of Skills, Training and Labour, 1995).

> *The Internet is changing the concept of publishing and new computer systems are being supplied with this in mind. Products like Microsoft's Windows NT server allow users quickly and easily to set up an Internet (Web) server: you can publish your own information – whether prospectus, article, poem, music or thesis – at low cost. . . Just as there was an explosion of books after the invention of the printing press, we can expect an explosion of digital books on the Net; the low cost and huge audience prove irresistible to anyone with something to say. (Highways to Learning,*
> 1995, 4)

In addition to a Windows NT Web server, faculty and students need a computer which can be connected to the server via telephone and modem, or direct network cable. The server, connected to the Internet, can in turn provide network connections to any machine attached to it.

Hypertext Markup Language (HTML)

One very important feature of the Web is HTML, the language that allows for the electronic publishing of documents containing text, animation, graphics, video, and audio. In the last few months Web or HTML electronic documents have become even easier to create thanks to a free add-on product offered by all of the major word processing software developers. Now anyone who can create and manipulate word processed documents can, with those same skills, create and manipulate hypermedia Web documents. For example, this document can be retrieved over the Internet from the Web home page, or electronically published document, located at Camosun College.

If this document had been electronically published on the Web, a mouse click on the following underlined word, Webs, would connect the reader to a Camosun College address (http://www.camosun.bc.ca/~buck) where the electronic pages of the Building Learning Webs project are stored and regularly updated. HTML permits, in addition to text, the electronic publishing of any multimedia event the web weaver has connected to this Web home page. For example, in a Web-based document the reader could use the computer mouse to click on an icon or picture of a speaker. In turn they could hear the author's voice played through the computer's sound card and speakers. As the Internet's bandwidth (capability of carrying data) increases, student Web users will also be to video conference interactively with their instructors.

Telematics – problem and solution

Educators are beginning to advocate the use of telematics to respond to the changing needs of adult upgrading students. Telematics can facilitate the development of instructional support systems to nurture the community of independent, self-directed, lifelong learners so critical to the information age. The information processing capabilities of the rapidly growing world wide connection of computers called the Internet offer opportunities for applying these approaches both within and beyond the four walls of the classroom. The British Columbia Ministry of Skills, Labour and Training (1995) announced a policy on information technology recognising ' that current and emerging educational technologies have special significance in the continuing development of the college and institute system.' The rub for post-secondary institutes in British Columbia is that all of the above must be completed '. . . within the existing resource allocation framework' at a time when increasing demands are being placed on educators to meet the needs of adult learners.

Towards effective use of telematics

What are some of the parameters for effective use of information technology in an Adult Basic Education context? Learners need a system that helps them feel self-confident and self-reliant as they use this technology to help achieve their educational goals. ABE instructors want sound andragogical (adult learning) principles applied in the use of information technology. They also want systems that will ease the clerical workload of testing, filing and the myriad other tasks involved with a competency-based system. Other stakeholders will be looking for a technology that improves a faculty's ability to structure information in new media and to new markets, so that student access to college programmes will be increased. For all stakeholders the most important issue will be the ease with which telematics systems can be modified to meet ever-changing instructor and learner needs.

Yet resistance to technological change can be found throughout history. After the invention of the printing press, perhaps people saw books as a way to do away with the elder who had passed on information orally. Will the same happen to today's teacher? Educational technology has yet to have a major impact on education outside of programming for mathematics and engineering use and more recently word processing. The number of teachers with little knowledge of the basic word processing skills remains high. Yet how much longer can educators resist this change? Changes in government funding mean that many educational institutions are facing reductions in funding. Ways must be found to increase instructor productivity if educational institutions are to meet ever-expanding demands. Some instructors also wonder about the role of the teacher in a technology-facilitated classroom. Does it preclude group work and interpersonal contact? They equate individualisation with programmed instruction and correspondence learning. However, once instructors experience this new refined role, 'away from that of transmitter and controller of instruction to that of a resource person to self-directed learners' (Knowles, 1981, 8), enthusiasm about their new freedom will surely follow.

Educational technology can also be as liberating for the instructor as it is for the learner. This is why some educators are attracted to information technology which promises even greater facilitation for debugging a student's learning and easing the clerical load of test correcting, filing and the many other tasks associated with an individualised programmes. Thus telematics promises the instructor greater opportunity and facility to meet with individual students and focus on their needs. That will only occur, however, as the power of the machine is put into the hands of the individual instructor and learner. The task of teacher as curriculum developer is to create curricula based on a new relationship between the human mind and the machine and thereby create 'a world made transparent by communications webs' (Illich, 1971, 157).

References

Axworthy, Lloyd (1995, April 12). Keynote speaker at *Leading Edge Training Technologies '95*. Conference. Victoria Convention Centre, Victoria, British Columbia.

B.C. ABE Student Outcomes Steering Committee. (March 31, 1995) *BC ABE Student Outcomes Report*. Vancouver, BC: Office of Institutional Research, Vancouver Community College

Cross, P. (1986). *Adults as learners*. San Francisco: Jossy-Bass.

Dede, C. (1989). The evolution of information technology: Implications for curriculum. *Educational Leadership*, 47(1), 23–26.

Goodlad, J. (1983, April). Improving schooling in the 1980's: Toward the non-replication of non-events. *Educational Leadership*, 4–7.

Goodlad J. (1983, April). What some schools and classrooms teach. *Educational Leadership*, 8–19).

Helm, D. (1995, September 12). Industry changes mean pink slips for 24 employees. *Times-Colonist*. B3.

Highways for learning – An introduction to the Internet for schools and colleges. (1995). [World Wide Web Home Page]. (British) National Council for Educational Technology. Available at http://ncet.csv.warwick.ac.uk/WWW/randd/highways/index.html.

Illich, I.. (1971). *Deschooling Society*. New York: Harper & Row

Illich, I. (1973). After deschooling, what? In Gartner, A., Greer, C. & Riessman, F. (eds.), *After deschooling, what?* (1–28), New York: Harper & Row.

Job-creation engine driven by 'small fry'.(1994, November 23). *Times-Colonist* , B11.

Kemp, J. E., & Mcbeath R. J. (1994, May–June). Higher education: The time for systemic and systematic Changes, *Educational Technology*, 14–19

Knight, Peter T. (December 1995). The Telematics Revolution in Africa and the *World Bank Group* [HTML Document] Paper Prepared for AFRISTECH'95 Symposium on Information Superhighways: What Strategy for Africa? Available at http://www.worldbank.org/html/emc/documents/afrirev.html

Knowles, M. (1981). *Modern practice of adult education – From pedagogy to andragogy*. Chicago: Follett Publishing Company

Kohl, H. R. (1976). *On Teaching*. New York: Schocken Books.

Lemke, J. L. (1993, April). Hypermedia and higher education. *Interpersonal Communication and Technology* [Electronic Journal]. Available on the Internet from IPCT-L@GUVM.BITNET).

Ministry of Skills, Training and Labour. (1995, Spring) Ministry Announces Policy on Educational Technology. *Contact@bc.ca*. Victoria, BC: Standing Committee on Educational Technology.

Papert, Seymour (1975). *Mindstorms : children, computers, and powerful ideas*. New York: Basic Books.

Perelman, Lewis (1993). *School's out : hyperlearning, the new technology, and the end of education*. New York : William Morrow.

Postman, N. (1973). My Ivan Illich problem. In Gartner, A., Greer, C. & Riessman, F. (eds.), *After deschooling, what?* (137–147). New York: Harper & Row.

Twigg, C. A. (1994, August) The changing definition of learning. *Educom Review*.

Chapter Three

Can you put your arm around a student on the Internet?

Jill Mannion Brunt

Throughout the history of adult education new ground has been broken in attempts to widen participation in education and create a culture of lifelong learning. The quest for informed and active citizenship has been at the heart of many adult education projects, often resulting in increased take-up rates amongst adults who have not traditionally participated in adult education. Traditional ways of working with adults have involved extensive periods of support, both on a personal level and an intellectual one. It comes as no surprise, therefore, that adult learning is now at the forefront of many developments associated with information technology. Access to open and distance learning through multimedia packages has offered opportunities to many adults who might previously have been denied their educational potential.

Perhaps the time has come to explore the impact of new technology on traditional methods of adult student support. There is no question that adults returning to study need support; there is, however, a need to recognise that support must continue to be offered, despite the medium in which teaching and learning takes place.

Practitioners in the field are aware of the difficulties that adults face if they wish to pursue an educational activity. Shift work or financial hardship account for many of these difficulties. Women in particular find that the caring responsibilities they may hold for children or elderly and sick relatives are incompatible with local education provision. This is often compounded in rural areas where the demise of public transport has resulted in many potential students becoming isolated in their communities. Recent employment trends suggest that women are increasingly active within the labour market, taking up part-time and shift-orientated work. Where their income may be the only wage in the household, even if time permits an opportunity to study, financial constraints become a pertinent issue.

Whilst many educational establishments are fast developing student support services to meet the needs of a broad section of the adult learning population, developments in multimedia teaching seem also to create new learning opportunities for adults. It seems ironic at times that organisations such as the Further Education Funding Council are expecting, quite rightly, high quality student support in further education institutions, whilst the very nature of adult learning may be undergoing massive changes. As colleges have set up well-resourced drop-in-centres, offering student support and guidance, some adult students will be sitting at home in front of a computer screen or perusing distance learning material. A different method of teaching and learning requires a different approach to student support.

There is no doubt that distance learning packages and interactive video are welcome developments and ones which will clearly bring more adults into further and higher education. However, the environment in which these changes are taking place can not be ignored if we are to continue providing the best possible learning experiences for adult students. The environment referred to consists of the typical characteristics of adult students, the current financial situation in terms of course fees and remission of payments and contemporary staff-student ratios. The opportunities offered by new technology should be considered within these parameters.

Many adults who return to some form of study do so with very little confidence. Many of them will have made the journey to education through community groups, voluntary organisations and trade unions. The journey will have been enriched by the personal contact and support that people give each other when they are members of such organisations. The discussions they have been involved in may have formed the basis for people developing confidence and discovering their potential for learning. The Ford EDAP Programme has been hugely successful in attracting working adults back to education, very often through peer group support and persuasion and a guarantee that people will not feel alone and isolated in the classroom.

It is not accidental or ad hoc that management courses are often organised around residentials; team building exercises are based upon personal contact and interaction, with people sharing ideas and responsibilities. Participants speak highly of the residential experience – a time to share ideas and experiences without the pressures of work or family; hence the enormous success of adult residential colleges. Discussion, debate, shared experiences and aspirations are all, it seems, an integral part of the successful adult learning process. We need, therefore, to consider carefully what a successful adult learning process will look like in the absence of these shared aspirations and interactions, in a multimedia world.

It is now widely recognised that some adults are extremely difficult to recruit back into education and that this may be adding to problems of long-term unemployment and to the lack of intermediate skills evident within the UK workforce. Much of the recent UK evidence suggests that in comparison to other European countries, many adults in the UK, either in work or unemployed, have significantly fewer educational qualifications. The problem is intensified within some UK regions and within some sections of the population, notably women returning to the labour market and men aged between 45 and 65.

Government agenda, the Department of Trade and Industry and individual employers have spoken forcibly about the need for individual commitment to learning and to re-skilling and educating the UK workforce (Taylor and Spencer 1994). There is an increasingly large number of adults for whom transient unemployment, low pay, short term contracts and poor training opportunities at work are a stark reality. For them, self directed study and distance learning do not necessarily offer them the kind of learning experience they need. Recent case studies in workplace learning illustrate the need for careful nurturing in the return to study process. (Forrester and Payne 1995). In areas such as South Yorkshire and North Derbyshire, people are still reeling from the effects of steel and coal industry redundancies. Their background and their culture is not one of high educational aspiration or attainment and they may be unlikely therefore to be switched on by the idea of self-directed study and multimedia packages. Practitioners working in the South Wales coalfields and areas around the South Yorkshire Dearne Valley speak passionately about the difficulties faced when attempting to recruit adult learners in these localities.

In order to achieve the National Targets for Lifelong Learning, a substantial number of these adults would need to return to some kind of learning. Given previous statements, it would be reasonable to assume that these potential students would require the maximum amount of interaction and personal contact and support, as they re-enter the world of education.

Some adult students often bring with them what many practitioners would term 'baggage': personal difficulties, financial hardship, lack of confidence and negative memories of their previous learning experiences – sometimes at work, but more often than not in relation to school. The fear that students bring with them is all-encompassing – fear derived from school, from redundancy, from so-called failure and fear even from thought itself. As Bertrand Russell so eloquently suggests,

' . . . if thought is to become the possession of the many, not the privilege of the few, we must have done with fear.' (Russell 1916)

The support offered to students in the first few weeks of their educational encounters is vital if this fear is to be dispelled. It is not unusual for a person's academic performance to be impeded by the difficulties they are experiencing personally and it is for this reason, amongst others, that many universities and colleges have set up student support services. As these services have developed it has become clear that a large proportion of the users are adult returners.

Anyone who works in the field of adult education will be aware of the huge potential that adult learners have to succeed academically and vocationally. Once they have committed themselves to study, they are enormously successful both in further and higher education. The educational opportunities which have been available to them have been underpinned by appropriate levels of student support throughout the learning process. As the distance between tutors and students widens through the advent of new technology and reductions in tutorial staff, an important element may be displaced or lost; one-to-one contact and the commitment and understanding which is inherent to this process.

Education has an important social role: the empowerment of people to question received wisdom. The discussion and debate which goes on within a seminar and tutorial is an important component when considering the skills people require in order to question such wisdom. The seminar and the tutorial have traditionally been the avenue for students to develop their intellectual and verbal skills. These skills are eminently transferable and we need therefore to consider their development within multimedia teaching. To neglect them would be to put students at an unnecessary disadvantage and may have implications for any future post-graduate work they may wish to consider.

Some adults require careful guidance through their learning experiences; they need encouragement and they need to grow confident in their academic and intellectual abilities. They need someone to talk to when their personal problems look set to threaten their academic aspirations. Taking control of their own learning is something which comes with experience, success and confidence. The Internet is adding a wonderful dimension to teaching, learning and research, but there is no substitute for putting your arm around a student with the words 'don't worry, of course you can get through it'.

Much is now being written about 'learner autonomy' and equipping students with the skills they need to survive in an ever-changing world. As practitioners we need to consider how we apply the concept of learner autonomy to new technologies in teaching and learning. Learner autonomy isn't just letting the student get on with it – there is a complexity around it which requires careful consideration:

'Different kinds of teaching and learning process can encourage or discourage it, but it does not depend on freedom from physical constraint, since it is an internal quality – a matter of how one feels about oneself, whatever the external limitations of one's situation. Nor is autonomy directly linked to isolation, an autonomous individual knows when and how to work with others and chooses when to be independent.' (Dept for Education and Employment 1996)

Practitioners should not therefore assume an autonomy within multimedia teaching and learning; the student may well have to learn new skills which will exist with traditional study skills and add value to the learning process.

Concepts such as the virtual college campus and virtual summer schools are discussed by Michael Tatlow in a conference report – *Flexible learning on the information superhighway*. He ends his report with the following statement :

' . . . we are at the beginning of the information age and educationalists must grasp the concepts and potential of the Internet and move forward with it rather than remaining static, because the World Wide Web is not a stationary creature.'

Quite so, but in the UK we should not lose sight of what is considered to be one of the biggest obstacles to social and economic progress – the high percentage of people with low educational achievement and the consistently high number of adults who have not been in a learning situation since leaving school. This is in spite of all manner of interventions from Government, the EEC and educational institutions. Whether or not multimedia teaching and learning will contribute to making good the deficit within this sector of the UK population remains to be seen.

This is not an attempt at an either/or argument; it is quite simply an alert to new developments which are gathering momentum and may offer new opportunities to adult learners. A student-centred approach starts with where people are and supports them through a number of stages. For some students multimedia packages are not a starting point for study – they may well be a destination reached along the way, but even then the student may require further support and guidance. The challenge for practitioners is to find appropriate methods of support which sit happily with new technology.

References

Forrester, K, Payne, J, Ward, K. Workplace Learning. Avebury 1995.

Russell, B. Principles of Social Reconstruction 1916; in Education for Democracy, Rubenstein, D and Stoneman, C. Penguin 1970.

Taylor, S and Spencer, E. Individual Commitment to Lifetime Learning. Employment Department July 1994

Living with Diversity: an executive summary of issues from the Guidance and Learner Autonomy Programme. June 1996

Chapter Four

The adult learner as listener, viewer and cybersurfer

John Field

New communications technologies are changing the educational landscape. Their advantages are, as the other contributors to this volume repeatedly demonstrate, both numerous and wide-ranging. Since the 1960s, plenty of people have predicted that telematics will completely alter the way in which we support learning. Sir Douglas Hague, for example, argues that developments in informatics mean

> 'that knowledge has become divorced from organisations and places. In future, people will use knowledge where it is, not where it can be institutionalised' (Hague 1996, 22).

In particular, telematics-based learning will be widely available because the technologies are familiar to us, and accessible to us, in our homes, our workplaces and our communities. Home-based technologies above all make it possible to learn with very little personal contact with an institutional provider.

Much of this excitement is reasonable, though it rests more on speculation than experience. The problem is that it tends to treat the learner as passive, as a recipient who absorbs the correct messages in a largely straightforward manner. Any breakdown in this process is usually seen as due to some defect either in the design of materials, or in the learner's ability to study. This passive model of the learner is entirely at odds with everything that we know about the way people actively interpret information and ideas depicted in the mass media more generally. In applying telematics to our learning challenges, therefore, we need to know far more about the ways in which the technologies are already being used in familiar settings such as the home.

This chapter looks at the ways in which the new opportunities created by informatics-based learning will have to take their place within a home environment that is, in its own ways, just as highly structured as and often more hierarchical than the average university or college. Adult learning does not take place in a social vacuum; rather it always has to compete with, fit into, and find meaning within the busy, messy world of our existing social relations, values and practices.

This chapter therefore explores:

- some contexts in which the new technologies are already being used for entertainment;
- some ways in which these contexts can influence the use of the new technologies in supporting learning; and
- the implications of both patterns for our approach to telematics in education.

I am particularly interested by the rapid development of the new technologies in the context of western consumer cultures (Field 1994). At present, firms constitute a relatively small market for telematics-based education and training. An expert committee convened by the European Commission speculated in 1994 that 'In Europe, like the United States, mass consumer markets may emerge as one of the principal driving forces for the information society' (High-Level Group on the Information Society 1994, 9). Rather, the major market so far has been individuals and families, and those who adopt the new technologies in order to exploit the fast-moving market for 'edutainment' services. For the producers of learning resources, the really big markets are those for home-based products. This is already visible in the massive public demand for educational videos, CD-ROM, and audio-cassettes in such subjects as gardening, motor maintenance or golf. Overwhelmingly, it has been the consumer market – generally not employers or education and training providers – which has created most of the new opportunities for telematics-based learning (Manchester 1995).

Consuming passions

Most people are familiar with some of the new communications technologies. Almost everyone has television; three quarters of all UK households have a VCR, and one quarter have a personal computer (Central Statistical Office 1994, 85). Some people use these technologies for home-based working, but they are a small minority. Most people experience the new technologies as a part of their leisure activities. This is one reason why education and training providers are so optimistic about the new technologies: most people who have them in the house think they are, or can be, a good way of having fun.

Part of the drive to apply telematics to education and training is its sheer accessibility. As the newer technologies expand into the home, so their potential to support learning will increase. Governments and the European Union alike increasingly recognise the significance of this development. As the UK government's Technology Foresight Panel on Leisure and Learning pointed out, the new technologies are bringing about a convergence between leisure and learning, for the following reasons:

- the same technologies will deliver both learning and leisure services into the home
- with more time out of work, leisure and learning will no longer be faced as an either/or choice
- providers are expanding into each other's territory (Technology Foresight 1995, 40).

Yet this familiarity breeds its own learning challenges. Above all, it encourages us to believe that the transition from consumer good to learning tool is a smooth one, and that the technologies themselves are somehow above the contexts in which real people put them to use.

Let me offer the example of television. Educational TV and video are now widely used, in schools, colleges, and universities as well as in distance open learning. Yet there are evident practical difficulties in asking people to switch from using TV for leisure to using TV as a medium of instruction. Think for a moment about what you are actually doing when you watch TV. A study of communications technologies in English households concluded that TV was 'intensely but unevenly used – often constantly on, it is not always watched intensely' (Silverstone 1991, 16). In an intriguing observation study of American viewers watching a 45-minute episode of a programme they enjoyed, Sandra Moriarty and Shu-ling Everett found that most viewers were engaged constantly in 'unrelated talking' – unrelated to the episode, that is. Most viewers used their remote controls to channel-surf ; under a quarter watched the programme without interruption to the end (more people actually switched to another programme part-way through). During commercial breaks, most people simply left the room to do other things (Moriarty and Everett 1994, 349–52). TV and video, in other words, fit into a wider pattern of social life. It would be strange indeed if people were to change habits simply because they are expecting to learn from this familiar medium.

Learners want to have fun

Providers of educational telematics products now see their consumer function as a powerful marketing asset. The BBC's commercial arm markets a series of educational CD-ROMs under the generic title of 'Fun School'. Manufacturers are not just treating 'fun' as an incidental feature, to be used in publicity. They also try to build fun into the curriculum. In 1966, the controller of education at the English Electric Company argued that TV and video were bound to affect the way that teachers worked:

> 'Professional entertainment has now reached such a pitch of technique that the educationist has to be effective to survive. For our task is not with those who have a love of learning for its own sake, who are only too willing to sit at our feet' (Lewis 1966, 7).

A decade later, the company Video Arts made its name by using actors such as the comedian John Cleese in its instructional videos. More recently, the director of the Institute for the Learning Sciences at North-western University, Illinois, claimed that his goal is to design multimedia programmes for 'the student who would rather be home watching television than be in the school'. His institute tries to design packages that will 'impart incidental information while engaging the user in a fun and interesting task' (Schank 1994, 5).

Having fun has always been an important part of adult learning. During the 1920s and 1930s, the workers' education movement was sustained by the common human bonds of what its active members often called 'fellowship'. Humour and sociability are particularly important parts of the adult education world because students mainly attend on a voluntary basis (Salisbury and Murcott 1992). Apart from any other reason, then, practical factors dictate that a good laugh can help produce positive outcomes, provided that we do not lose sight of the primary task in hand. My point is that we need to acknowledge that the contexts from which most learners will be familiar with the new communications technologies are powerful ones, which may well influence the way that learners engage with the ideas and information that are on offer.

These contexts are likely to have important implications for our approach to teaching and learning. For example, the strength of the consumer market for new technologies has helped create a range of products which do not require any understanding of the technologies themselves. The most obvious examples are the computing games of the 1990s; these are significantly different from the computer games of the 1970s and early 1980s, which required a minimal understanding of computing as well as keyboarding skills, and which could be (and often were) reprogrammed by their users. You can play extremely sophisticated games that do not require, or help you acquire, technical knowledge of any kind.

More broadly, the displacement of DOS operating environments by icon-based systems such as the Windows environment has reduced the need for personal computer users to know anything about the underlying principles of computing. This certainly reflects the demands of the market, which is for simple and easy-to-use systems. It also means that familiarity with the technology no longer requires any understanding of its underlying principles. This is likely to reduce quite dramatically the gains in informal knowledge by users, who can be completely IT illiterate.

There are risks in our tendency to overlook the blurred line between education and information on the one hand and entertainment on the other. A study of visitors at Welsh heritage sites shows some of the difficulties. For example, most visitors apparently rate audio-cassettes much more highly than they do display boards or exhibitions as a source of information about the site. Yet the audio-cassettes do not simply describe the visible remains and their history. What they present is rather like a dramatised history, with actors speaking from scripts in a fictionalised 'social history' of the site. It is hard to see how this can avoid trivialising the past, and encouraging merely a superficial understanding of Welsh history. Indeed, this is in some ways the point. Although the sites are publicly managed, the new technologies have become a way of gaining a competitive edge in what is now a fiercely competitive heritage tourism industry. Obviously enough a series of pedantic lectures or earnest displays, however well-informed by up-to-date research, will negatively affect the marketing effort; a lively and active multi-voice presentation is much more fun. However, our understanding of what is to be taught and learned is profoundly challenged in this process.

Bringing it all back home

Most people who are familiar with the new technologies will have used them in the home or in such family-based activities as shopping. Families are important contexts for learning. The home often provides the setting where most adults confront information and communications technologies on a daily basis. Roger Silverstone stresses that

> 'information and communication technologies, as objects and as media, enter complex and powerful social and cultural environments when they enter the home, and as such they are moulded by them. If they do not fit they are likely to be rejected completely' (Silverstone 1991).

At the same time, the new technologies increasingly permit the individualisation of home-based activities, separating the different members of the household in their cultural lives and often in their usage of space within the home. Educational activities are affected by these powerful influences just as much as any other application of the new technologies.

Families and individuals vary widely in their command over technological assets, as well as in their relationship to socially-distributed knowledge. These variations must be taken into account when planning and delivering learning support through the new communications media. We also need to remember that ownership of a particular medium does not necessarily mean that we know how to use it as a vehicle for learning. At least four major issues need to be taken into account.

The first point is that access to the new technologies remains uneven. Many commentators rightly stress that the new technologies are widely available within the home. This is true; but not all homes actually possess the new technologies. In the advanced nations, TV is pretty much ubiquitous, at least in principle. Most homes have at least one set; the important distinction is whether the home has two or more sets, so that family members can use them for different purposes (including learning).

Other types of technology are more unevenly distributed. In 1992 it was estimated that there was a home computer in 21 per cent of unskilled workers' households compared with 52 per cent of professionals' households; 91 per cent of employers' and managers' households had a VCR compared with 73 per cent of unskilled manual homes (Central Statistical Office 1994, 85). As well as the simple matter of possessing the hardware, the range and sophistication of the hardware also varies enormously. A survey commissioned for Technology Foresight showed that only 10 per cent of semi-skilled and unskilled workers claimed to have heard of the Internet, compared with 52 per cent of professional and managerial workers (Technology Foresight 1995, 100). By no means all adults, then, will be familiar with CD-ROM, the Internet, or even with a keyboard.

Second, access to the new media is also uneven within the family. Who gets to use the new media, and who decides who is to use them for what purposes? Current research into this question suggests that within many families the answers are complicated. One major British investigation (Silverstone 1991) identified the following broad tendencies:

- television is used intensely but unevenly by all family members, though at different times;
- male viewing tends to be concentrated while women tend to be constantly interrupted unless viewing on their own;
- computers are rarely used, other than for games (mostly by male household members);
- usually only one household member is able to programme the VCR, while others often refuse to touch it.

While it is an oversimplification to say that male adults always dominate family use of the new communications media, there are important differences between family members in the way that they access and use them. Gender is one particularly important dimension, and this implies that using any given medium – TV or video, say – can be a qualitatively different experience for men and women.

Age is another and perhaps even more important variable than gender. Command over new technologies tends to be strongly generational in nature. This is not quite the same as saying that it is related to age, though the two are obviously linked. What tends to happen is that any new technology is quickly learned by those who are relatively young at the time of its introduction. Even when the technology ceases to be new, like the telephone, some older adults can remain fearful or hostile. However, whenever a new technology comes onto the market, particularly if its spread is rapid, its users are usually relatively young. This pattern of dissemination tends to mean that new technologies appeal more to younger people than older adults. The study of the way audio-visual aids are used at heritage sites in Wales, for example, showed that older visitors felt uncomfortable with the Walkman technology used for audio-cassettes, relying instead on display boards and exhibitions for information about the site. Multimedia and computing manufacturers are sharply aware of these distinctions, and try to identify and then cater to the needs of different generational groupings, focusing particularly at present on the younger ends of the market.

Computing provides an excellent example of the problems that this pattern can create. Seymour Papert reports that many children see the computer as 'theirs':

> *'as something that belongs to them, to their generation. Many have observed that they are more comfortable with their machines than their parents and teachers are'* (Papert 1993, x).

This development, moreover, is taking place in the context of declining average family sizes, and a corresponding tendency to regard having children as a positive lifestyle choice. Some have called the consequences, partly ironically, the emergence of the 'infant king'. Certainly in areas such as computing (and even some of its simpler analogues, such as VCR programming), the possibility now exists of what some have called 'inverse socialisation': that is, the child knows more and is more skilled than the adults she or he knows, teachers as well as parents. Within the household, adults may have to seek guidance from children, who in turn see their peer group as the most effective source of relevant new knowledge (Cochinaux and de Woot 1995, 26–7). Even among young children, the ability to create, join and manage new social relations (or 'networks') becomes an important response to the breakdown of traditional socialisation agencies (Alheit 1994, 190–2).

Much less is known about ethnicity and language in respect of the new communications media.   In general, adult educators are paying increasing attention to the particular needs and experiences of learners from varying ethnic backgrounds, including those whose first language is not English. They have so far apparently given little thought to the influence of culture and language on teaching and learning through the new communications technologies. It seems likely that the growth of new communications technologies will pose this question much more sharply and urgently.

Terrestrial broadcast systems regularly transmit material in Welsh, Gaelic and Irish, though usually intermingled with predominantly English-language programming. The new technologies are creating new choices for non-English speakers; there are already cable and satellite channels which broadcast in Turkish, Hindi and Urdu, as well as in the main modern European languages; from 1997, the terrestrial Irish-language channel Telefis na Gaelige will be available outside Ireland via satellite and cable. One obvious consequence is that a great deal of informal learning will go on around these services; another is that they will test the market for other telecommunications services in languages other than English.

On the one hand, then, we can expect to see the growth of adult learning which is served by the new media in languages other than English. Some of it will meet demand in areas that are completely neglected by conventional educational providers – Islamic religious education, for example. On the other hand, the economies of scale imply that the range of materials in English will be far greater than in other languages, raising questions of equity and access for speakers of other languages. Yet much of this material will be produced by manufacturers in the USA or the Far East, raising questions of cultural barriers and relevance for native English speakers.

The European Commission has already expressed its concern over the longer term consequences – cultural and economic – of Europe's competitive weakness in the global multimedia software market. Yet in attempting to sponsor an educational multimedia industry, the EU is up against the limits posed to market growth by national and regional cultures, languages and traditions (including educational traditions). Ethnicity, language and culture have always been important elements in any educational system. The new technologies are raising these familiar questions in new ways.

Such an explosion of socialisation forces can too easily be celebrated as a new and welcome 'diversity'. While making the most of the new technologies' rootedness within familiar environments, we also need to acknowledge the tensions that this can create. Gender-based inequalities are only one part of the story, albeit an important one. Differentiation based on a combination of age, generation and life stage is also highly important. Thus Peter Alheit has noted the difficulties faced by educated daughters of working class families in Germany, faced with the need to negotiate the rapid detraditionalisation of their 'life world' (Alheit 1994, 186). The increasing use of information and communications technologies for education and training purposes intensifies an already contradictory set of channels of socialisation. While this certainly adds to the range of choices available to most people, it also opens up new prospects of risk, as well as (unintentionally?) increasing the potential for inequality and social exclusion. The challenge is therefore to identify ways of exploiting the new technologies for open, inclusive and democratic purposes.

Looking forward

None of this is to suggest that the new technologies should not be used in education and training, nor even that they are somehow second rate alternatives. For many people – particularly those living in remote rural communities, small societies or peripheral regions – distance open learning will offer an enormous improvement on the largely-absent conventional agencies. Yet even in well-provided areas, the new technologies will complement existing opportunities and open up important new ones. The purpose of this chapter is to emphasise that this will be a complex process, and we will have to take account of the real social, cultural and economic contexts in which adults will be learning to use the new technologies to acquire new skills and knowledge.

Specifically, then, there are several areas where we need to develop appropriate strategies. Readers might want to add their own ideas to those identified in this chapter, which include:

● emphasising inclusion, to ensure that the use of new technologies does not unintentionally condemn such groups as older adults, women or the unskilled to further exclusion;

● making learning how to learn a priority across all forms of adult learning, so that adults can exploit the learning potential of the new communications technologies to the full;

- using open venues creatively to make telematics-based learning available to a wider audience (eg through supermarkets, malls, cinemas and leisure centres);
- developing a strategic and inclusive approach to IT literacy, with a particular priority upon older adults, to ensure a minimum level of common knowledge between the generations and ensure that adult learners know something of the underlying principles which shape the technologies they are using;
- paying greater attention to media literacy within adult learning, so that learners have some understanding of the ways in which cultural representations and symbols are constructed within and mediated by particular cultural forms; building closer partnerships between private and public sectors and between the manufacturers and educationists, with the aim of ensuring that education and training goals are not drowned by entertainment-led production values;
- monitoring and evaluating the use of new technologies within a wide range of different kinds of adult learning;
- investigating systematically the complex interplay between identity, language and culture in relation to the new communications technologies.

Ultimately, an inclusive learning society will depend on these or similar measures. In their absence, market distortions will damage the ability of key groups of adults to participate and downgrade the quality of learning for many others. Technologies themselves will not bring about the required desirable changes; we need to understand and respond to the ways that they are used in real social settings such as the workplace and the home.

References

Alheit, P. 1994. *Zivile Kultur: Verlust und Wiederaneignung der Moderne*. Campus, Frankfurt-am-Main.

Central Statistical Office 1994. *Social Trends 24*. HMSO London.

Cochinaux, P. and de Woot, P. 1995. *Moving Towards a Learning Society*. Conseil des Recteurs en Europe/European Employers' Roundtable, Brussels.

Field, J. 1994. Open learning and consumer culture. *Open Learning*, 9, 2, 3–11.

Hague, D. 1996. The firm as a university. *Demos Quarterly*, 8, 22–3.

High-Level Group on the Information Society 1994. *Europe and the Global Information Society*. European Commission, Brussels.

Lewis, E.R.L. (1966) Industry and Adult Education, in *Adult Education in 1966*, National Institute of Adult Continuing Education, London.

Manchester, P. 1995. Home consumer market is leading the way. *Financial Times*, 7 June 1995.

Papert, S. 1993. *The Children's Machine: Rethinking school in the age of the computer*. Harvester, Brighton.

Salisbury, J. and Murcott, A. 1992. Pleasing the Students: teachers' orientation to classroom life in adult education, *Sociological Review*, 40, 3, 561–75.

Schank, R. 1994. Changing the Way People Learn. *Applied Learning Technologies in Europe*, 07, 4–7.

Silverstone, R. 191. *Beneath the Bottom Line: Households and Information and Communication Technologies in the Age of the Consumer*. Brunel University, Uxbridge.

Technology Foresight 1995. *Progress Through Partnership, 14: Leisure and Learning*. Office of Science and Technology, London.

Chapter Five

Teaching and learning with the new technologies: for richer, for poorer; for better, for worse . . .

Paul Helm

It has long been acknowledged that some of our thinking about the new technology is skewed by the fact that its detractors seem to be far outnumbered (at least in print) by its champions. Technology initiatives tend to attract the lone enthusiast. These enthusiasts have often spent so long enduring the long dark night of the innovator that they begin to lose sight of the blindingly obvious: subject specialists need to know more about their subject than about educational technology. There is a widespread suspicion in certain quarters that educational technology attracts peripheral figures, and that its use is still peripheral to most students' experience of learning. CAL, CBL, TBT, multimedia, the Internet, the World Wide Web and others can, at times, be all-too reminiscent of the King's new clothes.

Benefits

There is no doubt that teaching and learning with the new technologies require more effort than carrying on as normal. Using the new technologies is a huge learning experience for all participants. Moreover, even the most innovative staff are still 'mixed mode' in that they do not *always* teach using the new technologies, but still adopt traditional strategies as and when fit. Arguments about whether new technologies are a replacement or enhancement of traditional provision still continue; proponents of the replacement argument claim that the emergence of new technologies in education owes as much to the limitations of traditional education as to the benefits of the new technologies. These benefits are defined in different ways by different participants: management views are very different from those of tutors; tutors' views differ from students'. The Higginson Report on the use of new technologies in further education was explicit in its view of the benefits to be gained from a managerial viewpoint:

> *The investigation concluded that colleges are looking to new technologies and their applications to learning to help them to improve productivity, to manage planned growth, to help reconstruct the curriculum in modular and unitary forms, and to keep track of an increasingly heterogeneous student population.*

Tutors and students tend to see the benefits of new technologies in terms of *overcoming obstacles*. Obstacles arising from traditional provision for students include:

- costs, particularly for travel and accommodation
- disruptions to work flow and personal life
- rigidity of timing, duration and content

- the number of people who can participate
- possible irrelevance of much of the content to many participants

With costs coming down all the time, new technology would seem to offer the chance of a flexible, individualised curriculum.
Obstacles for staff include:

- limited access to equipment, requiring extensive forward planning
- technical support and appropriate training in the use of hardware and software are often lacking
- lack of confidence and time to develop familiarity

Many enthusiasts go all out for the replacement option – thus confusing students who may not be immediately aware of why the technology is being used at this point. Examples include course notes posted on the Web in a variety of formats (.DOC, .RTF, .PS etc) confusing to students, when all they want is hard copy. A tutor may not realise who they have to talk to about their intentions regarding, say computer conferencing – leading to libraries and computer centres coping with misinformed students or sudden increases in demand for certain services. This may lead to withdrawal – with the consequent effects on staff and student morale. Experienced practitioners try to slot the technology into the learning process as and when fit; for instance, a videoconference may be set up involving a guest lecturer whose script is circulated in advance and questions submitted before the videoconference to stimulate interaction; or computer conferences may be run on quite rigid lines, with introducers, summarisers, secretaries, etc in order to involve everyone in the conference. Many tutors now find e-mail indispensable to their day-to-day work – that doesn't mean to say their students will feel the same.

Staff development

Confusion is created when the better aspects of traditional and technology based teaching are not integrated – it is all too easy to see that the answer to everything is technological, and thus be tempted further and further away from one's subject discipline. Willing experimenters need to be aware of how hybrid their knowledge is becoming as they delve further into technology and how this changes their colleagues' perceptions of them – and there cannot be many tutors involved in innovative courses who at some stage or other have not had to get a screwdriver out or carry a load of equipment from one building to another . . . Tutors need access to a two-stage staff development programme. The first level deals with awareness and skills:

- raising staff awareness of the possibilities of new technology, preferably by listening to existing practitioners
- training in the use of the technologies – staff must be at least at the same level as their students.

The second level is concerned much more with the selection, creation, and use of materials using the new technologies, and would include;

- project management – many technological innovations in education are over-ambitious

● authoring skills to transform and adapt existing materials for the new technologies.

Even with a comprehensive staff development programme, some staff will still see obstacles; they may be reluctant to use materials developed elsewhere; they may have concerns about copyright and intellectual property; they may be resistant to changing their role. These obstacles are addressed at the end of this chapter.

Evaluation

Evaluation cannot be tacked on at the end of a project, it should form an integral part of the whole teaching and learning strategy. Evaluators must first decide what to measure, define the instruments of measurement, and then measure the efficiency and effectiveness of the project. Innovative projects need innovative evaluation techniques.

At Bradford we attempt to measure the effectiveness of the technology in assisting learning through a variety of measurement instruments including focus groups, interviews, real time observations, and questionnaires. We collect more qualitative data than quantitative data, in line with our objective of illuminative evaluation. This emphasises the more qualitative aspects of evaluation and has more in common with ethnography and social anthropology. Illuminative evaluation strategies are less likely to take any predetermined stance and ought to be flexible enough to change in the light of experience gained during the actual investigation – it uses observation, interviews, discussion, informal conversations etc to establish what the people most concerned think and feel about the course, curriculum, and institution involved.

Most of the current work in the field deals with educational effectiveness: advances in evaluation techniques are becoming a major by-product of the Teaching and Learning Technology Programme (TLTP). We have to be very careful not to impose models and criteria from inappropriate examples; it is worth noting that much of the TLTP work is based on foundation level courses in mainstream Higher Education, and does not focus on some of the most important issues for adult learners coming to technology. All learners, but especially adult learners do not arrive without preconceptions, they bring with them, amongst other things:

● different levels of prior knowledge
● different conceptions of the subject domain
● different study styles
● different study modes
● different personal objectives.

Illuminative evaluation offers a means of discovering competing interests among the various actors involved in the teaching and learning process. Quantitative evaluation, however, is necessary for measuring efficiency and perhaps cost-effectiveness, and is bound to play a role in summative assessment. Perhaps the key question for us would be, 'is teaching and learning with the new technologies as good as, or better than the traditional methods – and why?' To this end, we follow a framework of needs analysis, formative evaluation, and summative evaluation.

Needs analysis (preparatory evaluation) means talking and listening to learners and immediate past learners, tutors, and, if appropriate, employers, to explore factors influencing motivation such as expectations.

Formative evaluation measures progress towards achieving programme goals during implementation. When a project utilises new technologies, this stage can all-too easily turn into monitoring the technology. The risk with all such projects is to allow the project to be driven by the technology rather than by the teaching and learning issues. Students often work in unexpected ways with prototypes – they indulge in unprogrammed interaction – and we need to concentrate on the educational aspects of the evaluation as well as the technology. I remember watching students working through a prototype CD-ROM-based economics package that kept crashing (as is to be expected of a prototype). It was our original intention that each student should have their own machine – because of the technical problems they ended up sharing the machines that actually worked. We were intending to evaluate the package's usability, the effectiveness of the interface. As the students worked in groups, and we fretted over the technical problems, we nearly missed the fact that the students obviously preferred working in groups with the materials. Indeed, each group had arranged themselves in identical formation around the machines; the mouse and keyboard were shared around the group with metronomic regularity; and the level and quality of interaction with each other and the materials was heartening. These observations altered the goal of the whole project – we decided to try to replicate the quality of the group interaction by increasing the functionality of the package (in this case, by using videoconferencing and application-sharing for remote group work). This is how it should be – students first, technology second.

Summative evaluation is usually aimed at assessing the effectiveness of a programme on completion, aiming to answer questions such as *'Were the aims achieved?'*, *'Was it worth doing (this way)?'*, and *'Is it worth continuing?'* Often this part needs expert opinion, anyone who has been involved in innovative projects will know that you can get too close and lose the wider view.

Findings: advantages and disadvantages

Advantages

- most students feel that the technology can be a helpful addition to traditional systems. Praise is given to guest lectures given by videoconferencing, the Internet as a research tool, e-mail as a way of contacting tutors – all equivalents for real life events and actions
- a substantial proportion of students like to work in small groups with the technology and help other students to use the systems; they feel they learn more by showing others
- students being in control of their own learning and greater flexibility are mentioned most frequently as plus points
- technological features such as video clips in multimedia or Web access (to sites such as the Vatican Library or foreign language news agencies) are mentioned as being *realistic* as opposed to academic
- learning to use the new technologies has a knock-on effect on general IT skills
- a constant theme is that the technology can help students use their time more efficiently, there is less likelihood that they finish working before they intended to.

Disadvantages

- reading from a screen is deemed to be less effective than reading from paper
- even though many packages try to simulate traditional systems, features such as Notepads are unpopular. There is a general feeling that paper-based materials allow you to have more information in front of you.
- there are many worries about navigation – the novelty of hypertext wears off quite quickly if you are pressed for time or have an assignment to complete.
- a secondary problem with navigation concerns the variety of interfaces used – students often worried if they were using the package in the way it was designed to be used.
- the more you know about Windows, the better you seem to do with Windows-based learning materials
- video clips and videoconferencing were often described as gimmicks – the quality was deemed poor
- many students felt there was just too much jargon involved; computer experience questionnaires, essential for gauging the level of expertise, were seen as threatening and confusing.

Overall, the answer to whether teaching and learning with the new technologies are as good as traditional methods is . . . it depends on what it is being used for. *Different* is a word that occurs time and time again in our evaluations. Interviews have shown that students mean different things by different: sometimes for adult students it means that the new technologies make them work in different ways (with the implication that they are uncomfortable with the different way); other times they mean that the experience does not meet their expectations, and they obviously feel like guinea pigs. Sometimes, however, they are enthused by the difference – the technology fits in with an image they have of what should be happening in education in the late 1990s. Though some of the disadvantages are clearly technical and will ultimately find technological solutions (video quality, better interfaces, and search engines for instance), some of the problems are to do with the way the various participants interact with the technology – the final section outlines possible developments.

Added value?

Using the new technologies in education can tempt some to conflate what is essentially a delivery system into an educational philosophy (thus mirroring the confusion between open and distance learning). An example is multimedia, which tends to come as two extremes: at one end of the extreme are the large databases with 'user-friendly' front ends and search engines (what might be described as the Encarta or edutainment model); at the other extreme are electronic books, where the main interaction is often to click on a symbol to move to the next page. Both extremes include some measure of hypertext (to give the learner the illusion of freedom?) Yet the use of multimedia for anything beyond foundation learning is problematic. The new communications technologies offer a way out of this 'spacebar mesmerism.' The World Wide Web, the Internet, and videoconferencing promise to take away the solitude involved in learning with technology by offering interaction with peers and tutors. One of the greatest virtues of computers is patience – no matter how many times you get it wrong, you can always try again. This patience is rather inhuman, however, and the promise of contact with your (real as opposed to virtual) tutor should enrich the learning experience. At the moment technology-based teaching aims to either replace or enhance the learning experience, and this often leads to evaluations that try to discover whether the innovative method is better or worse than the traditional method. This seems to miss the point – students feel technology-based teaching is different first, and better or worse second. It is this difference that suggests that a new form of literacy is in the process of formation – it includes basic literacy, but also an understanding of the grammar of film and TV, of the process of browsing through hyperlinks, and the ability communicate effectively with the new communications technologies. This latter is not to be underestimated; it may be true that e-mail has revived the art of letter writing, but isn't e-mail a rather attenuated form of communication where speed is the dominant feature and emotional nuances very difficult to read?

Some aspects of traditional delivery can transfer across, others cannot: the formal lecture can be delivered via videoconferencing or digital video on a CD-ROM; a tutorial, where the debate is continued over coffee with the tutor and other students who happen to be around, cannot. I believe that the new technologies will give birth to new ways of teaching, but remain reluctant to jettison all of the traditional approach.

Interaction is one of the most widely abused and ambiguous words in the educational lexicon. Definitions exist for open and distance learning, attempts can be made at outlining the parameters that mark out flexible learning from resource-based learning from student-centred learning – but all the time, active learning and interactivity are assumed to be widely understood. Interactivity can be used to mean communication between two or more people; in the context of multimedia, it often used to refer to the students' ability to follow hypertext links or stop and start video clips. As Mason points out, 'much of what passes for interactivity should really be called 'feedback' – and the temptation with multimedia is to have a rather attenuated feedback (typically yes/no, continue to next screen, multiple choice questions which are marked by the computer). The educationalists, then, are convinced of the value of interaction; students, it seems, are less concerned – even though they **insist** on interaction. This paradox of insisting on opportunities for interaction yet not using the opportunities may well be a product of prior learning experiences or, more likely, a failing on the part of tutors to fully grasp the potential of the technologies, often combined with a lack of resources to match their intentions.

New technologies: new learning?

Teachers

The single most powerful determinant of the successful use of new technologies in education will be the creativity of individual teachers and the strength of their desire to improve their courses. The context of learning and support services must be designed to promote and support this creativity. In the last few years it has become commonplace to refer to teachers as 'facilitators', over the next few years, they will move towards becoming learning managers, learning resources, and eventually, as learners begin to manage their own learning, information brokers. The potential of the new technologies will never be fully realised unless they are fully integrated into provision, and the critical success factors are as follows:

- management commitment to the importance to the new technologies
- high expectations on the part of management regarding teachers, learners, and the technologies
- ease of access for teachers and learners, at college and at home

Embedding technology into teaching and learning does involve a leap of faith, not least in trying to optimise the learning environment. Presently, technology-based teaching is a cottage industry: if it is to fulfil its potential, it will become industrialised. The days of teachers as courseware authors are all but finished – in future their input will be content and pedagogics. Multimedia is not inherently educational, at the moment it merely presents information without meaningful interaction; the new technologies will not work if we merely attempt to replicate existing practice through them. Educational technology is at the same stage now as film was at the beginning of the century – the first films were made by pointing a camera at a theatre stage. The first fruits of new technologies are usually more and more of what was possible with the old technology, and multimedia and communications are no different. We will see real interactive learning when teachers become confident with the technology, and are sure of their role in relation to it. Advances in communications technology are going to lead to new ways of learning – teachers have to be part of the process of discovery, otherwise the old dictum will hold true: if you're not hands on, all you get is hand outs.

The focus has to shift from acquisition of the technology to changing the culture(s) of the institution. Teachers have to have a greater focus on how learners learn: the emerging context of learning means that teachers will pay greater attention to prior knowledge of learning; detailed preparation of the learning task(s); the different approach learners adopt; the learners' perception of the assessment; and, the logistical factors. Teachers and learners should know the answer to the question, why use the new technologies here? If the answer is not obvious, the technology is bolted on. All too often, a simplistic equation is made that new technology is the answer to increasing workloads and numbers of learners, as well as the decreasing unit of resource. The real solution to the latter is for teachers to look to adapt rather than create, to drop the 'not invented here' syndrome, and to collaborate with colleagues in their own college and at other educational establishments. Teachers should be pursuing professional development in the area of network skills, pedagogics, and of course, content knowledge.

Good teachers will remain good teachers whatever methodologies they use. Enthusiasts are dangerous if they chase the technology and become technology-driven. Most educational establishments are poor at disseminating good practice, those that improve will gain competitive advantage. Network skills, skills in adapting courseware and worldware (see section 3) are crucial. Those who do not embrace the new technologies will have it thrust upon them.

Learners

In the next few years students will begin to manage their own learning with total freedom to choose modules from any institution in the UK and abroad. Network skills will be crucial to independent and flexible learning – network literacy will become as important as other forms of literacy. Tracking systems will be important to stop open door policies from becoming revolving door policies; to stop self-paced learning becoming no-paced learning. Whilst there will still be a top-down emphasis on quality, most learners will rely on informal guides and assessments from previous learners (this is already happening with the news groups on the Internet). Learners are already using the new technologies as sources of information, and institutions that do not offer on-line courses, school/industry links, and support across networks will become invisible beyond their immediate environs. Only a small proportion of learners actually want the totally virtual college – most can see the benefits of social development and interaction and peer stimulus. Interpersonal skills will become even more important to avoid isolation and deal with the shorter lifespan of groups. Access will remain a problem with some groups, and there will always be a need for Learning Resource Centres (LRCs). The real challenge is to transform the LRCs firstly into places where learners do more than word process, and then into Intensely Supportive Learning Environments (ISLEs) and, if that is achieved, to make those ISLEs accessible by distributed groups of learners.

Examinations and possibly grades will disappear. New technology will be used initially for tutorial support (asynchronous moving in time to interactive), and remote assessment of competencies. Modules will come in a variety of lengths and delivery methods. As now, learners will value support systems as highly as, if not higher than, learning materials. Institutions with high quality support systems will attract learners. Whereas now, learners may buy a textbook that comes with a free disk or CD, in the near future the book will be the freebie. Network skills will move beyond keyword searching to encompass the use of agents and new forms of software called mindtools that will sift information.

Technology

The pace of change in communications technology is much faster than developments in stand-alone PC technology. In order to avoid chasing the technology, institutions will have to anticipate changes from an educational standpoint and base their strategy on perceived present and near-future needs, balanced with delivery constraints. Whilst we are all looking forward to the possibilities that broadband will bring, such as two-way instantaneous transfer of video and data, the reality is that most companies will expect to have intermediate bandwidth, either through cable connections or ISDN, for the next couple of years. It shouldn't be forgotten that narrowband still has valid educational uses, such as computer-mediated conferencing. Services aimed at different client groups will have to take account of the variations in bandwidth – we are probably looking at a mean of 10Mb/s by 2002. By 2002, it is to be hoped that the market becomes more market-driven as opposed to the current supplier-driven scenario.

Providers will move away from time-based tariffs. Levels of ownership will rise, (but the PC will not be as ubiquitous as the calculator). There will be more legacy machines. Hardware will begin to include connectivity tools as standard, eg modem, videoconferencing unit. Problems with IPR will lead to fewer suppliers of courseware rather than more, and these will be commercial enterprises (perhaps in partnership with colleges). Courses will be a mix of courseware and 'worldware', the latter describing what we now know as personal productivity software being used in an educational context – put simply, the spreadsheet is the best problem-solving tool invented; most courseware is a database in some form or another. Student editions of commercial software are already popular: there will be an explosion in their growth as they mutate into mindtools.

Ten years ago, I had never touched a computer – I found electronic cashpoint machines confusing. Six years ago, I began teaching adults how to use computers – out of 60 people who completed my course in 1990 less than 10 owned or had access to a machine. This year I would estimate that 7 out of 10 students on the course own or have access to a machine (sometimes of a better specification than the machines in the classroom). 18 months ago, nobody had heard of the World Wide Web – today, it is hard to find someone who hasn't. The pace of change is frightening and exciting – frightening in the sense that I have to throw away so much of my materials every year; exciting because I am beginning to realise that I must begin to use the new technologies so my materials are not instantly fossilised.

References

Draper, S W et al (1994) *Observing and Measuring the Performance of Educational Technology*, University of Glasgow, TILT TLTP project

Gunn, C (1994) *Designing and Evaluating Effectiveness in CBL: Defining the Problem and Designing a Solution* unpublished paper from TLTP CLASS project at Heriot Watt

Hamilton, D et al (1977) *Beyond the Numbers Game: A Reader in Educational Evaluation* London

Mason, R (1994) *Using Communications Media in Open and Flexible Learning* London

Martin J, Darby J, Kjollerstrom B eds (1994) *Higher Education 1998 transformed by learning technology* Oxford

Report of the Learning and Technology Committee, (1996), the Further Education Funding Council

Teaching and Learning in an Expanding Higher Education System, (1992) The Committee of Scottish University Principals

Thorpe, M (1993) *Evaluating Open and Distance Learning* London

Notes

[1] Report of the Learning and Technology Committee, 1996, the Further Education Funding Council, (Annex D para 16)

[2] Scriven B (1991) 'Distance Eduation and Open Learning – Implications for Professional Development and Retraining' *Distance Education*, Vol 12, No 2

[3] Mason, R, Using communications Media in Open and Flexible Learning (1994) London, 25

Section Two

Chapter Six

Adult learning by videoconferencing

Alan Robinson

'Monday night is my adult class,' and Philomena leaves her Irish-speaking friends in a mountainous townland in rural Donegal for urban Derry just across the border in the UK. At the same time, over 100 miles away, Claire leaves her English-born friends in Hillsborough in County Down for the leafy suburbs of Jordanstown just across the other side of the city of Belfast. Philomena and Claire live in different worlds in the same historic province of Ulster and are divided by history and politics, but both are enrolled on the same part-time course at the multi-campus University of Ulster – and they learn together.

Context

The mission of the University of Ulster is to meet the educational demands of the whole community. A videoconferencing system was installed on three (later four) campuses in 1990: Magee College in Derry; Coleraine; and Jordanstown (Belfast was added in 1995). It replaced an unpopular audio-conferencing link and, to the surprise of many, has been well- received by adult students. Good quality sound is the most important element of an effective interactive educational technology but vision has made all the difference.

As well as providing access to courses normally restricted to the immediate environs of a distant campus, and reducing the travel costs of those who might have been prepared to drive quite considerable distances, this form of telecommunication can guarantee course viability. Adults can register for the same course at their nearest campus where they attend the same class taught by the same tutor. When videoconferencing bridges the cultural distance between Philomena in the west at Magee and Claire in the east at Jordanstown, it is operated by their tutor on the third campus at Coleraine in the north.

Six years on, an upgraded videoconferencing facility is used by tutors to deliver a range of courses to another campus, to deliver joint course elements to another institution in Great Britain and, occasionally, to draw on expertise located on the continent of Europe and beyond.

Benefits for adult learners

One particular application of videoconferencing to adult teaching and learning has been in the field of cross-cultural and cross-community understanding. Philomena and Claire's learning has resulted in a greater knowledge and understanding of themselves, of each other and of the traditions that they represent. Student evaluations have shown consistently that class members appreciate the wide range of backgrounds and interests among them.

When the adult class is spread around four videoconferencing classrooms there is a greater diversity among the background, the opinion and the aspirations of its members. Not only have classes provided an integrated education for Catholic and Protestant, but the means of delivery has facilitated an educational experience to challenge all traditions or groups, Nationalist and Republican, Unionist and Loyalist and none of these. In their attempt to comprehend the Northern Ireland 'troubles', once they have become familiar with the videoconferencing classroom, Donegal students have told their classmates in Down 'to wise up' and the Down students have said that those in Donegal 'should catch themselves on', but no offence has been given in the secure setting of the videoconferencing classroom.

The application of videoconferencing to link two groups of the Channel 4 'Talking Heads Club' in Northern Ireland, meeting at The University of Ulster at Magee College in Londonderry and at Queens University, Belfast, has highlighted further an equality of opinion among members from different backgrounds. For instance, the views of the retired bank manager in Belfast are balanced by those of the small farmer in Derry on the issue of Europe. The potential benefits of videoconferenced learning for mutual understanding among ethnic groups and international understanding are apparent.

The members of all adult classes learn most effectively through interaction and, if used to its capacity, videoconferencing need not restrict learning for those located at a distance from the tutor. On the contrary, videoconferencing can enhance learning but this 'value added learning' will depend on the willingness of tutors to develop an appropriate pedagogy.

Experience at the University of Ulster suggests that classes have three parts to them; this provides a model for teaching and learning in the videoconferencing classroom.

- Adult classes generally begin with a short presentation by the tutor who will provide explanations with the help of graphics transmitted by a rostrum camera. This is done via a vertical camera at the side of the tutor's desk and is comparable to the conventional OHP. An extraordinary zoom facility can transmit many rediscovered 35mm slides and video-clips can be shown most effectively and without any disruption to the flow of the presentation. Given the opportunity, and some 5–10 minutes of basic training from the tutor, class members have shown themselves quite capable of contributing short presentations of their own.
- The second part of the model will be a period of campus-based independent group work. This allows the adult class to interact as three separate groups, to co-operate on a given task and to engage freely in dialogue without the interference of the tutor! In order to avoid being distracted by noise emanating from the other campuses, the sound volume (or indeed the picture monitor) may be turned off. A telephone link to the tutor is available in case there is any uncertainty, but if the task is carefully planned or prepared it is unlikely that the tutor will be contacted.
- The third part of the model for adult teaching and learning by videoconferencing will be interaction that is cross-campus. With the tutor as chairperson, the dialogue allows group and individual feedback and opinion to be shared or exchanged and for values to be clarified. Some myths may be exploded in the process.

This three-part model of presentation, independent campus group work and cross-campus discussion may be used to structure most classes building up to units or modules of study. In the examination of controversial issues it can accommodate cross-campus simulation and role play activity, which not only distance issues from immediate reality but also provide a deeper insight into them before the follow-up discussion.

If interaction at this level is to be successful on accredited courses experience has shown that participants must meet together in a face-to-face setting at the start of the course. This means that students are required to express their willingness to travel on at least two occasions. All participants have stated in their post-course evaluations that this contact and meeting together is essential if the psychological distance between strangers is to be bridged by videoconferencing at a later stage.

Value-added learning

Some former participants with an educational role themselves have come to use videoconferencing in their own work. For example, contacts arising from town-twinning arrangements have been followed up by videoconferencing and language students from an Irish border town at the North-west corner of Europe have benefited from cross-national French conversation classes with the continent. University staff with European partners from informatics, business and management and modern languages or who are required to support students on European placements are also finding videoconferencing of benefit, but the bulk of academic staff faced with large student numbers on their own campus have no necessity to adopt it. Indeed, when the writer offered to do a short course on how to teach by videoconferencing to the Staff Development Unit in his University (1993) there was insufficient interest shown to proceed with it.

Some interest has been shown by a small number of other institutions in Ireland and in the UK and demonstrations have been provided for visiting groups interested to see videoconferencing for themselves. One of these was the forthcoming University of the Highland and Islands of Scotland.

Adult students who are in a position to avail themselves of EU student mobility schemes increasingly will be supported on placement from their home institution. Tutors will find that not only is this more efficient but also they will be spared the problem of work that accumulates during their absences away from campus. Plans are also being made to further develop the European dimension of several courses. This will promote increased levels of international understanding among adult learners who may also use computer conferencing to supplement videoconferencing use. It may not be long before Philomena and Claire will be able to continue their studies together and be joined by Marjetta from Finland and Armando from Spain.

Practicalities of using modern communication technologies

Some students have expressed an initial fear on being 'put on the spot' in videoconferencing classes, but the source of the problems in teaching and learning by videoconferencing are technical. Before the equipment was upgraded in 1995 there had been some difficulty with sound quality. Ceiling microphones required participants to lift their heads unnaturally high away from their notes on the desk top and it was common to request that something be repeated. Mobile microphones on stands and desk top microphones have, of course, improved matters.

A medium-sized monitor fixed immediately below the camera focussed on the tutor and showing the distant student body was also a welcome modification as it meant that the tutor could see who he was addressing as he spoke to the camera. Without it, the tutor was required to look away from the camera lens and down at a small monitor below the tutor's desk.

The University of Ulster's videoconferencing facility is 'technician-free' in that once the equipment is checked in the morning the tutors are left to get on with it. Should breakdowns occur a telephone link may be used to raise technical help. As technicians finish work at 5.00pm the equipment is checked once more for night use. It is fortunate that in general the system has functioned satisfactorily at night. The writer has had to complete a very small number of classes by sound only but loss of sound has not been known to happen since the early years of use.

Conclusions

The experience of some five years application of videoconferencing to the teaching and learning of adults in the University of Ulster has identified a number of principles:

- Videoconferencing is a means to the ends of effective adult learning; tutors must be interested in the pedagogy that enable their students to learn. Currently, the technology is 15 years ahead of the use that educationists make of it and tutors can easily be seduced by it: effective adult learning cannot be technology-driven.
- Tutors must induct their students into courses delivered by videoconferencing and into its unfamiliar classroom: insecurity or fear never did promote meaningful learning.
- Before videoconferencing is used to deliver a course with an element of cross-cultural understanding adult students must be willing to have face-to-face contact with one another: one cannot see eye-to-eye unless one has been face-to-face.
- Tutors must plan adult learning in creative, experimental and varied ways; they should also reflect on their practice and focus on specific action steps to improve performance. Tutors returning to more conventional classes can benefit from the transfer of competence highlighted when teaching by videoconferencing.
- Courses delivered by videoconferencing are required to be evaluated from the measures of distance education rather than from those associated with face-to-face delivery. Tutors normally come from a conventional background but they cannot expect teaching by videoconferencing to simulate what they are used to. Learning by videoconferencing is not a second best; it is different.

Where next?

The telecommunications industry has moved on and computer conferencing might capture the imagination of educational technologists and users, but cross-campus and cross-institutional videoconferencing within and between nationalities allows adults to learn in groups. As cuts bite deep into university education, the adoption of the videoconferenced classroom provides a possible answer for some educators to the increasing squeeze for efficiency in the delivery of learning. It promotes distance education and a dual mode of delivery among tutors with a conventional campus background.

University organisations, however, have themselves to learn that the adoption of videoconferencing requires their academic staff to be provided with adequate technical and pedagogical support.

Chapter Seven

Developing videoconferencing: the East Anglia distance learning initiative

John Smith

City College Norwich (CCN) is a relatively large College of Further and Higher Education which, in April 1995, was successful in a funding bid with three other colleges (West Suffolk, Cambridge and Peterborough) to install and run high specification videoconference facilities. The project was supported by British Telecom.

The major thrust of the three-year project, the East Anglia Distance Learning Initiative, is to research, through practice, the role of videoconferencing in post-compulsory education and training. Each college appointed a project manager for their site, and the project as a whole is managed by a representative steering committee. The backgrounds of the site managers varied from significant experience of IT and media work to virtually none: the author of this piece was in the latter group and what follows here reflects his experiences of the first eight months of the project from the particular viewpoint of a technical novice managing one site in the consortium. We could have benefitted from the experiences of others in education who had made mistakes and learnt from them: this is intended to help those just entering videoconferencing to avoid a few pitfalls.

Setting up

Since all the partners were new to videoconferencing, BT provided valuable advice in the early stages about equipment, premises and connection to their ISDN network which was, almost in its entirety, followed by the colleges. Consequently, four BT VC5000 series studio videoconferencing cabinets were purchased and installed (running at up to 384 Kbps on 3 ISDN2 lines) together with recommended premises modification and peripheral equipment. At CCN we debated whether to purchase a display camera but are very pleased we did as it allows a variety of inputs to the remote ends. One BT multi-point conference unit (MCU) was also purchased for the consortium and installed at CCN: this allows up to eight sites to be connected simultaneously. BT desktop VC8000 systems were also purchased and installed at colleges in preparation for outcentre developments. The initial set-up period was planned to take four months; in fact, by November (eight months in) the main studio systems had been running for about six weeks and the bugs were still being ironed out. There seems little doubt that, in planning your installation lead time, as with your holiday spending money, you should always plan for twice as much as you think you'll need!

The room at CCN housing the studio system was chosen because it was:

- in a relatively quiet part of the college,
- large enough to seat thirty people and house the video system
- near enough to IT Services to easily enable technical support and

- one of the least politically sensitive rooms to use (don't underestimate the importance of this)!

It had removable blinds placed at windows to allow use of the room for non-video work (very important in FE for space utilisation purposes), air conditioning (a really worthwhile investment for comfort) and an inner lobby built for privacy and soundproofing. The recommended curtaining was purchased (we have since found that we could have used a different supplier at half the price and we really don't need all the curtaining we installed) and all other modifications made, some of which are more useful than others (for instance, it is essential to have a separate telephone line in the room).

When possible, try to take advice from those in education who have first-hand experience of videoconferencing. This is not to decry BT's contribution in our project; on the contrary we needed their advice particularly for the ISDN connections and MCU use since our connection set-up with the MCU was not straightforward. There is, however, a growing band of educators who are willing to share valuable experience of various systems and different combinations of equipment. As more equipment suppliers enter the market, I suspect this will become more important.

One of the desktops was installed in what was previously a small store cupboard to provide another facility for up to three people. This was modified again with air conditioning, curtains, etc, and is currently used to provide:

- an essential ability for remote staff training into the studio (even though it's literally only 10 metres from the studio the impact on staff of the trainer potentially being in New York is impressive!)
- a small videoconferencing facility to avoid tying up the studio unnecessarily
- an opportunity to examine the potential of shared applications on desktop.

Another desktop system is about to be installed in a sixth form centre about thirty miles from the college to be used both by students there and for remote work by the college. This installation is currently giving a little cause for concern due to lack of a secure location: the equipment used for desktop videoconferencing is very easily portable yet expensive so it's worth considering placing it in either a secure room or, in a case such as this where you want easy access to the room at other times, in a lockable cabinet in the room. We have also been experimenting with a modified desktop system and a high quality PC projector to combine shared applications (which are in general available only on desktops) with access by a large audience. This has the added advantage of allowing use of the projector for normal teaching purposes at other times.

The rooms at CCN are booked mainly on a first-come first-served basis by IT reception who also rigorously enforce our restriction of allowing only accredited (ie, trained) users. Because the videoconferencing was set up in close liaison with the existing IT services the rooms have been available and technical support forthcoming all the time they are open is (0830–2100 and some weekends). The same provision may have been available had it been set up with the existing Learning Support Services (who support our 'media' provision) but the crucial lesson here is to make sure videoconferencing is strongly supported by an existing service: those who set up independently seem to suffer ultimately. There is some advantage in setting up with those who control both computing and telephony. The need to use the room for other than videoconferencing (we agreed use for meetings, tutorials and small seminar groups, but try to avoid regular teaching in there) has been a source of conflict: if it's possible to agree a dedicated room, do.

Staff development and usage

Our staff development programme was based upon two related facts. The success of videoconferencing in further education is largely dependent upon the support of teaching staff and the studio equipment we installed required a certain level of competence for use. We decided, therefore, to restrict unsupervised access to the studio to those staff who had undergone a training programme and, because most people don't really know what you're talking about when the term 'videoconferencing' is used, we offered a three-tier development programme.

First was a one hour 'familiarisation' session providing for groups of up to eight staff with the aim of simply providing experience of videoconferencing. They may get to press one or two buttons but the hour was spent mainly discussing the potential of the system, seeing it working and participating in a live conference. Our aim is to offer this to all staff (over 1,000) by December 1996. This was followed, for anyone who wished to sign up, by 'training in usage' which comprised a two-and-a-half hour session for up to six staff at a time during which they would receive instruction in the use of the equipment followed by seven hours of shared practice. After this they were listed as 'accredited' users and could have full unsupervised access to the studio. The project manager provided all the sessions in the early stages but soon familiarisation sessions were provided mainly by accredited staff. The final stage of staff development will be a fuller exploration of teaching and learning techniques which is being pursued with colleagues in the consortium at present.

Part of BT's contribution to the project comprised free call charges for the first period. This was crucial to the success of the initial phase since we didn't have to worry about the cost of the activity so used it freely. In the main, staff were very impressed with the links, particularly to colleges abroad, and it was often difficult to get students out of the studio at all!

In general, people have warmed to the medium after the initial five minutes of embarrassment. Our experience indicates that the quality of the audio is crucial to the success of the conference: people will put up with poorer quality video than audio. It is strongly advisable to set up a telephone link if you have any doubts about the reliability of the video link: there were times (admittedly not many, but one is enough) when the video link proved unreliable either for technical reasons or because we were not sufficiently skilled to iron out faults. The inevitable time delay in communication has not proved any barrier for us. On 384 Kbps it is not really noticeable in point-to-point (that is one end talking to another) and at 128kbps in point-to-point it has not interfered unduly. In multi- point (that is more than two ends connected at once) it is necessary to conduct proceedings as you would a very well ordered meeting with a firm person chairing. It is crucial that the chair is very strict in inviting each site to contribute at the point the chair determines and makes it clear from the outset about the conventions to use (such as a site stating clearly its name and nothing else in order to be invited into the conversation). There is no doubt whatever that videoconferencing has improved the communication skills of people because it's harder to interrupt, you need to be more succinct in what you say and, above all, you have to learn to listen!! Rather than facilitating mainly remote lecturing as we expected it has been the interaction which has been most exciting to see develop.

The use for the options provided by the equipment has proved to be variable. Some systems seem to provide facilities which, whilst exciting, have limited value: for instance we rarely use the 'preview' facility except for demonstration purposes; we probably wouldn't miss the dual screen; and the ability to move cameras remotely in Tokyo, whilst exciting staff and students, really has limited value compared to the main use. Conversely, we are very pleased we invested in a good quality document camera and we are making a few modifications to improve our facility such as another camera in the studio to allow us to vary our video input, repositioning the microphones to improve lecturer speech and we are considering how to allow people at the back to see the incoming screen through the heads in front!

The future

The next stage of the project will see a whole raft of joint curriculum developments building upon the current work. These include:

- pre-GNVQ students doing joint project work
- beauty students giving demonstrations remotely
- a jointly-delivered qualifying course in credit management
- a journal for media studies students
- shared work on new standards in hairdressing.

Staff are forming groups to examine shared assignments and implementation of new standards and the opportunities for working with colleagues in other colleges both here and abroad are really beginning to excite some staff and students.

The current use for administration and management to save travelling to meetings and enhance normal telephone contacts will increase: as CCN is part of Anglia Polytechnic University with campuses up to 90 miles apart the potential here is high.

The next year will see a growth in our desktops being installed into local schools and other centres for purposes of remote teaching to support students with tutorials and specialist lectures who cannot travel every day; also to teach whole courses. The relationships we are already forging with other colleges all over the country mean we are likely to become involved in drawing on expertise for our students which was previously denied and also providing it for others where we have it. The rapidly increasing use by industry and commerce means they will also have expectations about their training provision.

How all this pans out in the bigger world of college finances and competition is still to be tackled but there is little more certain than that this steady march of technology will continue to affect teaching and learning to provide our students with increasingly exciting opportunities.

Chapter Eight

Video links and outreach centres

A L Leal

'People really do find the material easy to use and the whole learning process great fun – even those who are tentative to start with. They soon learn how to use the computers and the video link. The great thing is that we are giving opportunities to people, many of whom are unemployed, to learn a skill in their own areas without the need to travel or even move away' (David Stanbury, Director of Enterprise Tamar, who hosts one of the Outreach Centres).

The following case study describes the use of video links and outreach centres to deliver training to clients unable to visit a traditional training centre. This might be because they are disabled, from a rural community where there are transport problems, have family and domestic responsibilities or because of prohibitive travel costs.

The system described is capable of delivering training to the customers rather than bringing the customers to the training and, at least in theory, can provide training in any particular area.

How did the venture start?

The seeds of the project were sown seven years ago. With the declining number of 16-year-olds the Business Studies Department organised a one-day conference with representatives from various women's groups to ascertain what the more mature student required from college. At the end of the conference the message was that they wanted courses which started throughout the year, allowed flexible attendance and gave the opportunity for students to work at their own pace.

At the time the College had no such provision. In response to these identified needs a pilot Open Access Centre was established with 12 machines and materials written for two packages, a word processing and a typewriting package. The immediate success of the pilot resulted in the number of machines being doubled; within five years there were 100 machines and a quarter of a million pounds had been spent on developing a totally flexible centre. The staff had also increased the range of materials available, so that at the current time there are over 40 separate courses on offer.

The centre is now open for 50 hours a week (including Saturdays), 50 weeks of the year. Students can start at any time, work at their own pace and choose their hours of attendance.

Four years ago we were approached by a group representing disabled and disadvantaged groups to see if we could provide flexible training for their clients. The decision was made that we would utilise the materials developed for the Open Access Centre and develop a pilot with modem links. As a result of the success of the pilot we now recruit 75 people a year.

Three years ago a group of existing customers to Open Access, living in Bere Alston (a small village approximately 15 miles from Plymouth) asked if we could set up an Open Access Centre in their community. Given the size of the village this would not have been viable: instead we decided to operate a pilot using our Open Access materials with a (then new) video link called Picturetel. The success of this led to the establishment of another outreach centre at Launceston and further provision throughout Devon and Cornwall.

We now have ten centres spread throughout Devon and Cornwall with over 90 computers, each with a CD drive and a Sharevision system, which provides each computer user with a direct link to the main centre at Plymouth. A successful bid to Regional Challenge, with the University of Plymouth, will develop another 40 centres and add satellite and information services to all the outreach centres.

Each centre operates in the same way as the main Open Access Centre at Plymouth. A student can enrol for any course on offer, start when they like, attend when they wish and have as long as they need to complete their course. There is a communications room adjacent to the Open Access Centre in Plymouth which is staffed for 30 hours a week (with two staff at busy times). These members of staff are solely for the use of the outcentres. If any student has a problem they call into Plymouth to talk to their tutor. If necessary the tutor can then take control of their computer (or CD), give the student a lesson and then allow the student to demonstrate that they have understood the lesson before they hang up and then continue working through the packages in the outcentre.

As will be apparent, the video links are not used for video conferencing in that we do not run classes through the video links. The customers are quite adamant that they want to attend at times convenient to themselves: having timetabled classes obviously renders this impossible. For that reason we can use Sharevision which operates off BT lines rather than an ISDN system. Although Sharevision does not give us video conferencing facilities, it offers all the other facilities normally available through an ISDN system and as we do not use video conferencing the reduced cost, and greater flexibility, of Sharevision has made it the obvious choice.

What do the customers think of it?

Good indicators are success and retention rates. At one outcentre there were 116 registrations between 1 September and 1 April and of these only 17 dropped out. The pass rate of those remaining was a staggering 97 per cent. Our current projections indicate that there will be over 1,000 enrolments from the outcentres this year and almost all of those will be taking courses leading to examinations. In order to develop this provision we had to overcome a number of problems:

Technology

In our first centre at Bere Alston we used an ISDN 2 system. Whilst this worked extremely well, there were the costs of installing and then renting the line, with the latter being the real problem. Establishing outreach centres in small communities means that there will be a limited number of students using the centre each year. While this does not pose a training problem in that the tutors at Plymouth service a number of centres, this obviously means that the cost of rental has to be borne by very few users. This was clearly a disadvantage. A further problem was that if we decided after a period to move equipment to another community then the cost of installing the ISDN line had to be written off.

For this reason we moved over to Sharevision which is a video system which operates on BT lines. This means that the system can be installed anywhere where there is a telephone and has the advantage of being mobile. We are therefore not only using the system in outreach centres but also in the homes of the disabled. After one term when they have completed the course and passed their exam we simply move the system from one person's house to another. Having selected Sharevision there have been a few problems. The technology works well; although when there is a force 9 gale and the telephone lines are carried overhead there can be difficulties!

Materials

Where trainers use videolinks to run traditional courses, materials do not provide a problem: as indicated above we aim to provide individual programmes for clients which are totally flexible. Such programmes depend on high quality materials. We were fortunate in that we had a large bank of materials which had been specifically written for the Open Centre, but we have had problems expanding the range of courses that we can offer both in the main centre at Plymouth and at the outreach centres.

The technology exists to produce high quality training material in CD format. Unfortunately there is very little (almost no) quality training material leading to external examinations in the UK. In the main centre we are currently piloting CDs that we have obtained from the United States in languages, construction, numeracy, literacy and IT. If these are successful then we will be able to add to the range of courses available in the outreach centres. We are also developing our own CDs in the Business Administration field. Currently we employ four authors (three of whom are on secondment from the University of Plymouth) to develop materials in this area to be launched in Autumn 1996. Hopefully similar initiatives will mean that the range of offerings within the Outreach Centres can be increased. In order to access funding from the Further Education Funding Council all our courses lead to national qualifications.

Finance

Capital   At the time of going to print the cost of each computer plus Sharevision is approximately £2,200 and therefore the cost of setting up an Outreach Centre with 10 machines is around £22,000. A few years ago funds were available for innovative projects; once established these were capable of generating income which could be used to open new Centres. For anybody starting now raising capital will be a problem, particularly in view of the reductions in government funding. Nevertheless, there are sources of funding available which we are currently tapping and anybody who is enthusiastic enough will usually find a way of raising the necessary funds.

Running costs   In the College it is necessary to have staff available whenever the Outreach Centres are open. If a customer has a problem then they need to talk to their tutor immediately. If they have to wait because, for example, the tutor is not available until the following day, they are likely to vote with their feet. Staffing a communications room for 30 hours a week is expensive and therefore requires a minimum number of enrolments. With 10 Centres and 1,000 enrolments we have the funding.

It may be that there will be a loss in the early years unless it will be possible to find a creative way of providing staff support. The bad news is that in addition to having to fund staff in the main Centre a contribution towards the cost of the Outreach Centres is also needed. In the early Outreach Centres we relied on volunteers; this caused problems and restricted the number of hours the Centre could be open. As a result we now try to work with Centres where there is an existing infrastructure, such as a Community Centre. If there is a manager, secretary, caretaker, etc, this will ensure that the provision can be open for 30 or 40 hours each week and because the staff are already employed within the Centre running costs are reduced.

Selecting Outreach Centres

There will be no shortage of organisations wanting to become Outreach Centres; the problem is selecting those that will be viable, both in terms of setting-up costs and then running costs. When establishing a Centre it is very easy to overlook basic items such as security. If you go into, for example, a village hall with no security it could cost several thousands to make the premises safe. In a rural community the income generated by enrolments is not likely to cover this cost.

It is also necessary within each Outreach provision to have some form of secretarial support because somebody needs to hand out the materials and be available to collect them in at the end of the clients' training session. Again if you have to pay for these costs you may find them prohibitive. There are also other costs such as who will provide the counselling, who will complete the enrolment forms, who will complete the examination entry forms and, perhaps most important of all, who will undertake induction with new students.

Within the Outreach Centres there are varying approaches to the solution of these problems and it is likely that given the varying sizes of Centres this will always be the case. The ideal solution is to be able to generate enough income through enrolments to be able to pay for a member of staff to be available in the Centre for a given number of hours each week. The students would then be told that whilst the Centre may be open for 30 hours a week they can only go for counselling and guidance when the specialist member of staff is available. Having counselled and then enrolled them on the appropriate course the students would then attend for their first two or three sessions at times when the member of staff is available. He or she can then introduce them to the packages and start them off. When the students have problems the member of staff would not be there to solve the problems but to ensure that they became familiar with the VideoLink to the main Centre in Plymouth. Once the students are capable of using the VideoLink without assistance they will then be encouraged to attend at hours when the member of staff is not available. This of course may not be possible in the smaller Centres where one is still likely to be reliant on volunteers or the goodwill of other people who are already working in other parts of the building which hosts the Centre.

Delivery

Having overcome the technical problems using the VideoLink and developing the materials the provider then needs to satisfy themselves that the following are in place:

Initial counselling and induction   At the main College site this is performed by academic staff who are present in the Centre. Obviously this is not possible with Outreach Centres and therefore unless it is being done over the VideoLink which would be both time-consuming and expensive it needs to be undertaken by staff in the Outreach Centre and the suggested solution has been outlined above.

Devising the necessary administrative support   The materials in which the students work are probably expensive. It is therefore necessary that they are handed out at the beginning and collected at the end of each student training period. It is necessary to work with the Outreach Centre to ensure there is storage near the training room and that a member of staff who is in the Centre will be available to dispense and collect the materials.

Marking   As there are no teaching staff in the Centre it is necessary to provide a means of marking the students' work so that they will have feedback prior to their next session. This can be achieved by the students sending down their work to the main College Centre using the Video system. It can then be printed out in the communications room, marked and returned to the students before their next session.

Examination entries   As most of the examination Centres are not examination Centres in their own right it is necessary to devise a system whereby students can enter for the examinations.

Tutorial support   Without which the whole system will fail. So far little mention has been made of potential problems with staffing. This is because we didn't have any at Plymouth! When we initially investigated the possibility of Open Access some seven years ago I had over 50 full-time staff. Of these, four were committed to the concept of Open Access. They were responsible for the initial pilot with 12 machines.

It soon became apparent that this was going to be an enormous success and then other staff wanted to join the team. Since then the Centre has expanded and the range of packages and the technology used has evolved to keep up-to-date with modern developments. Because of this the Centre has been able to recruit its own staff who are not only committed to the concept of flexible learning but also have the necessary skills which might not automatically be present in an existing lecturer.

Anybody seeking to start from scratch is unlikely to be in the same position and is likely to require a substantial staff development programme. Even then the staff involved must be committed. Any attempt to impose flexible learning on reluctant staff will lead to the situation in which another College has found itself. They obtained funds to develop VideoLinks and given our expertise, asked us to become involved with them. Having set up their system it then transpired that in all their Outreach Centres formal classes were being offered with a tutor conducting lessons in a classroom. The VideoLink was used so that the tutor in the Outreach Centre could talk to the tutor in the main College! The staff did not believe the training could be offered flexibly through materials utilising a VideoLink and therefore were carrying on with formal classes, thereby rendering all the expenditure on video equipment totally pointless.

Given the potential problems, why bother to do it? With the current financial problems of further education, offering flexible learning in Outreach Centres provides substantial income for the College which enables the purchase of modern technology and remit staff for the development work. This gains staff approval. Those working on this venture have won two national prizes (NIACE – best use of technology – and the Beacon Award For Distance Learning) and will also have come to the attention of the chairman of the corporation.

The main reason for doing it, however, is that there are now 1,000 students throughout Devon and Cornwall who without the VideoLinks would probably not have had access to any training at all. Where better to finish than with some quotes from existing students?

'I don't think I really had any expectation of gaining any experience given difficult financial circumstances, a very active two-year-old son and no equipment to use at home. You can imagine my astonishment when I discovered that all these difficulties could be overcome with home based training. I was able to fit the entire course around the family without exhausting and expensive journeys to and fro and I didn't even have to worry about childcare for my youngest son' – Linda.

'My initial reason for wishing to study was to stop myself from vegetating as I have not worked since my illness five years ago. I was particularly interested in the computer course as this has also opened up the possibility of obtaining home-based employment some time in the future. I have found the course fast, clearly presented and easy to follow. The VideoLink has transformed these courses – the ability to make instant visual contact with a tutor who can have access to (and take control of) a file on my own screen has proved particularly helpful in this respect' – Ian.

As indicated the clients think the system has proved successful but as Ian said there is one main drawback 'I now have to ensure that I look presentable when I sit down to work!'

The future?

Mention has already been made of 'RATIO', the successful bid for Regional Challenge funding. Since this bid was submitted technology has moved on and this is why predicting the future is so difficult. I am not a technologist. I merely use technology to deliver training. In the future I don't know what technology we will use but I do know that we will be able to offer training to customers anywhere and at anytime. Whether it be through the internet or digital TV is immaterial as far as the customer and trainers are concerned. Technology is merely a means to an end.

Chapter Nine

Low-cost computer-mediated conferencing for part-time evening degree students

Kate Sankey and Dominic Dibble

The integration of new information and communications technology in teaching and learning is a field which requires energetic resourcing. This is not just a question of large amounts of funds for hardware and software – although this may help! It is more a matter of staff awareness of the possibilities and limitations of the technology. There is considerable concern within the University that software which is already available could be better applied to the benefit of the student's educational experience. A project within the Teaching and Learning Technology Project (TLTP) has addressed this issue and has supported activities which focus on the opportunities for 'value-added re-use' of existing technology. This may refer either to educational software specifically designed for teaching a particular subject, or in the case-study outlined here, exploring the educational potential of communications technology (Computer Mediated Conferencing (CMC) software, Internet and World Wide Web (WWW)). CMC refers to software which allows students to input messages to a shared discussion area where they can be viewed, organised and responded to. As a result there is a permanent record of the group discussion.

The University recognises that improving the information technology (IT) situation will require encouraging staff to think more innovatively when designing, delivering and evaluating courses, as well as becoming more familiar with what IT has to offer as a teaching and learning technique. This entails the complementary skills and interests of understanding the practicalities, possibilities and limitations on the technical side together with the particular educational aspirations and objectives which can be enhanced through the application of IT. In our particular case we saw an exciting chance to explore ways of integrating CMC into the experience of part-time adults studying on an evening undergraduate degree programme in Environmental Education. This group is seen within the University as particularly disadvantaged since they are physically isolated from the student body except for a three-hour session once per week.

A fruitful link was made between the Department of Educational Policy and Development and the VARSETILE[1] project at the University which enabled a small amount of funding to support a Research Assistant. This was an important element since the project therefore had access to dedicated staff time to this aspect of the course – essential to ensure that a good idea does not fall at the inevitable first practical or technical hurdles.

A course in Environmental Education calls for seeking out all manner of techniques which encourage student engagement in dialogue with the subject material, tutors, and fellow students. Thus we were forever asking ourselves questions such as: What is it about CMC which could enhance the student's learning experience? What different aspects of learning are taking place? What is the 'added value'? Does the technology get in the way of the learning?

This case study deals with the use of networked computers and some readily available free software to permit CMC for students on a part-time evening degree course whose access to one another is more limited than full-time students. It was felt that CMC could provide a forum in which students could develop ideas in response both to the course content and to each other, thus setting up a fruitful educational dialogue. This use of CMC thus has something in common with uses in distance learning – ie, facilitating access to others' ideas, while at the same time being set in a context where students did have limited access to one another. Incidentally students were also gaining confidence in using the technology itself and basic keyboard skills.

The majority of students taking this course are adult returners. The wide variety of backgrounds was expected to enrich the dialogue in the conferences. Consequently there was a very wide range of computer literacy, which naturally raised issues of IT training. Several sessions were dedicated to training and this was provided in contact sessions, with references available on-screen and as hand-outs.

Educational objectives

The CMC software was used as the medium for three different educational techniques:

Collaborative writing ('asynchronous tutorial'). Autumn semester 1994. Students were presented with a theme to debate. Each student was asked to contribute a piece and the 'tutorial' developed through subsequent entries which pursued different key issues with additional supporting evidence brought to the debate from student's own experience, readings, the Internet and tutor's comments. The objective of sharing all this information using CMC was to enable students to reflect and comment upon each others' position and thus to generate a dialogue. Each student was assessed on the quantity and quality of their contributions. One of the main criteria for the success of threads was the amount of dialogue generated.

Journals Autumn 1994, Spring 1995 and 1996. Students were asked to record their developing perceptions of the units. They made critical reflections of the course material and consolidated their understanding through relating concepts and principles to their own personal or corporate experiences. Since they had access to others' journals there were a number of instances where reference to one another's experience helped clarify a position.

Community of inquiry Spring 1995 and 1996. This is a rather specialised form of group discussion activity ('conference'), initially developed by Matthew Lipman (1991). Essentially it is a framework within which a group can follow a line of inquiry which is group-led and involves all members. The inquiry is generated by a stimulus material which is used to evoke questions concerning a controversial issue. In the initial trial (Spring 1995) this was the group's own journal material and more recently (Spring 1996) we introduced the international element with two readings (one put forward from Scotland and one from Australia). From this starting point the group negotiate the key points at issue, and as a community move the conference forward. Thus the conference does not have a stated end point other than the exploration of whether there are some points of mutual agreement and affiliation.

The first and third of these are explicitly group activities which benefit from being pursued over a number of weeks. The second is also one which is often used over the duration of a course, and it was felt that giving all students access to each other's journals would help to enrich the experience. The students reacted positively to the introduction of these techniques although when the technology let us down, or there were serious difficulties of access to computers, there were the inevitable cries of frustration and always a danger that the technology might get in the way of the educational objectives. Where students struggled with access to computers this was most acute.

Training of students was essential and several dedicated sessions within the early weeks of the course were required to get them going. The Research Assistant was also available as a trouble -shooter and to co-ordinate the developing contributions. We did not use any manuals or training texts: rather, materials were purpose-made with instructions and simple tasks to introduce the application.

Software tools

The original idea as conceived received considerable modification as various technical and resourcing constraints and conditions became evident. The project team were learning on their feet and it was important for such developments to remain flexible and adaptable.

Initially we used a *Usenet Newsreading* package, with local newsgroups set up to provide the site for the computer conferences. There was a disadvantage in that the newsgroups were local to Stirling University and access from outside was extremely limited. We then moved on to using a WWW browser, where the 'conferences' were set up on Web pages which were created by students sending e-mail messages to the Research Assistant who acted as a moderator and co-ordinator. He then inserted messages onto a Web page and was able to organise the entries and include comments from tutors. This permitted easy viewing and participation from outside Stirling. In the most recent development of this project the Community of Inquiry conference went international. A group of students of Environmental Education at Griffith University, Brisbane, worked alongside the Stirling students with significant international dialogue taking place. Using the Web enabled much greater flexibility and variety of presentation. Graphics and photographs were included and hot links between contribution made the conferences very much more dynamic.

Usenet

Problems   *Usenet* is not a package which is specifically designed for conferencing: there is no mechanism for linking themes and organising messages into sub-topics, which is possible with more sophisticated conferencing software. We found that the software was not very user-friendly; moreover students had to be familiar both with *Usenet* and the Web browser in order to take advantage of the wealth of information available on the Internet.

Solutions   Students were asked to identify sub-themes so that contributions were recorded under different 'subject headings'. Thus they had to decide what the issue was which they were addressing before sending the contribution. All contributions with a given subject heading were listed together which on occasions resulted in rather contrived titles with little flexibility, and thus some themes 'dried up' whilst others contained a vast amount of discussion and debate.

For those students who had special difficulties, extra training sessions were arranged. This was offered on demand and was only possible due to the flexibility of the Research Assistant (a recurring theme – the importance of energetic and enthusiastic staff commitment)!

World Wide Web

Problems   Initially *Mosaic* was used and latterly *Netscape*. Both are very user-friendly systems with occasional difficulties experienced in navigation to Web pages where the conferences were located, due to inaccuracies in typing. The home page for the Spring 1996 unit was http://www.stir.ac.uk/epd/env_ed/

The main functional problem experienced was that of information overload for the co-ordinator. This was most obvious in a recent unit with 18 Stirling students and potentially 25 Australian students sending e-mail messages each week to the Community of Inquiry. Consequently, the greater flexibility of organising messages wasn't fully exploited; equally the opportunity for tutors to comment and advise on the journal entries was confined to twice per semester and assessment was a lengthy process.

Solutions   There is no simple solution to this particular problem, other than looking for the appropriate balance between the amount of contributions generated by the assignment and the availability of time from the co-ordinator and the tutors. We suspect that the demand made on the students was too great given their access difficulties.

Hardware

The computer networking facilities of the University of Stirling were initially used to set up the *Usenet* conferences, hence any student who could gain access to a computer on campus could input information. External access was difficult and indeed there was only one case where a student working at a different University was able to access the system remotely. This was not ideal, as it meant students travelling into the University. Using the WWW browser extended access, so that in theory any student with access to a computer linked to the Internet could e-mail messages to the co-ordinator. If the student had access to a WWW browser they would also be able to read the conferences. This is still not ideal, since there were wide disparities in access, thus contributions varied between students. Equal access would almost certainly produce even better results and would enhance the student's experience, but would require students with home computers or easier access through their work, library or local educational institution. Other hardware problems included a couple of major network crashes which of course is a hazard of working with technology which is beyond one's control.

Resulting student experiences

The use of CMC is believed to offer a new domain of learning: Harasim (1990) claims that it is 'much more than a technical device for exchanging information, computer conferencing facilitates the sharing of knowledge and understanding among members of a group who are not working together at the same time or place'. This was largely confirmed by the students' experience. One student wrote 'on the whole I feel that the facility to share information and to read each other's work-in-progress has helped to bring out information and stimulate reflection on the course that wouldn't otherwise have happened.'

All three activities produced interesting results. The most recent course has yet to be evaluated but the international dimension was certainly seen as a valuable additional extension. The students readily accepted CMC as a valid educational tool whilst accepting the pilot nature of the project.

Collaborative writing Autumn 1994. Unit: The Environment and Society. The debate theme chosen was Vegetarianism. The theme brought out a lot of the course material and prompted discussion which was wide-ranging. Various Newsgroups on the Internet were used to bring opinions and information to the conference. Students recognised the need to gather information from a wide number of sources including the Internet, and made good use of the extended time frame of the conference – returning with additional information or seeking out corroborative evidence. Students who invested time in visiting other locations for data collection and general interest commented on the constraints of time. It is all too easy to spend several hours 'surfing' and if this includes international links then the time for 'connection' can be frustrating. Students were warned! Students were willing to question each other's ideas and the resulting contributions had considerable depth and insight. The style of writing was quite informal with students being prepared to give interim opinions: 'my argument is still in the making'; 'I see most problems related to the environment controlled by the science of economics. Do any of the group think my view is too limited?'; ' I was thinking about food chains recently, and the energy flows in the farming biostructure, the less links in the chain the more efficient the whole process'.

Journals Autumn 1994, Spring 1995 and 1996. The greatest use of journals was in the The Environment and Learning Unit. Here students were required to make an entry every week. Many students adopted a personalised style using phrases such as 'I believe . . . ; in my opinion . . . ; it is my hope that . . . ' Students did relate to other people's journal entries offering support and agreement on some aspects. Of the three activities, however, the use of CMC as a delivery method for journals was the least critical, although there were a number of instances where students commented on each other's entries.

Community of Inquiry Spring 1995 and 1996. Unit: The Environment and Learning. The nature of the technique lent itself well to CMC: in the first year an inquiry was started from material from the student's journals. The group then successfully picked up on a number of themes; discussion then ranged with some or all of the group responding. CMC is no substitute for a face-to-face real time discussion, but the nature of an inquiry is such that there is a time lag as new evidence is brought to the table, as and when required. Sometimes the progress was disjointed but perhaps this must be simply accepted as a different way of conducting a discussion. Certainly the opportunity to extend the Community of Inquiry to an international level gave us a clear justification for this method. The students found this added dimension particularly interesting and exciting. The results of the latest work have yet to be analysed but it would appear that CMC is indeed a different domain of learning, allowing students a different experience of communication and dialogue.

Conclusions   In spite of access, software and hardware problems indicated above, virtually all students succeeded in inputting interesting material, and the dialogue component in collaborative writing and community of inquiry successfully emerged, with some students making very intelligent use of this. The actual form of the communication reflected the informality of the medium allowing some students an easier structure in which to discuss and debate.

Experience suggests that these educational techniques are worthy of developing and that the IT should be fine-tuned as a medium for delivering them. As more course material is provided on the WWW and more students have remote access to Higher Education, it is essential that techniques which enhance group interaction and collaboration are developed. The technology now available must enhance and not dictate the educational experience, and encourage people to develop the skills of critical and informed thinking as people competent for the multi-faceted world of the 21st century.

References
Lipman M, (1991) *Thinking in education*, Cambridge University Press, Cambridge.
Harasim (Ed) (1990) *On line education: perspectives on a new environment*. Praeger, New York.

Notes
[1]Value Added Reuse at Stirling of Existing Technology In the Learning Experience (VARSETILE) supports and facilitates the reuse of hardware and software for student teaching and learning and its evaluation. It is one of the TLTP projects supported by the Higher Education Funding Council

Computer conferencing and the continuing professional development of teachers in the post-16 sector

Tony Lewis, Maude Gould and Malcolm Ryan

The School of Post Compulsory Education and Training at the University of Greenwich is the country's biggest provider of pre-service and continuing professional development for lecturers, tutors and trainers in further and higher education, in adult and community education, and in vocational training for the public and private sectors. Its largest single course is the part-time Certificate in Education/Post Graduate Certificate in Education for serving staff, and in the 1995–6 academic year over a thousand students registered for this programme at the 11 centres where it is offered. Since 1993 a distance learning version has been available, and more than 50 per cent of the current students have chosen this mode of study.

The course
In order to gain the full teacher's certificate students have to accumulate 120 credit points, usually 60 at Credit Accumulation and Transfer Scheme (CATS) level 1 and 60 at level 2. Most course members devote two years of part-time study to this, although a substantial number enter directly into level 2 with advanced standing for a City & Guilds 730 or similar award. The level 1 units, by and large, are expressed in competence terms, while the level 2 units are more directly instructional and discursive. Each completed unit gains 15 credit points.

Teaching on the distance mode is delivered through a series of interactive printed texts, written by members of the course team and mediated by personal tutors; materials are posted to students at the beginning of each semester. Distance students are required to attend either the University's centre in the City of London, or an alternative designated centre, for three separate days during the year: an induction day in September; a revision day towards the end of Semester 1; and another assignment preparation day in Semester 2. In addition, personal tutors make teaching performance (TP) assessment visits to each student's place of work, and in most cases regular communication takes place over the phone and by letter.

The problem
However, the disadvantages of studying in this way have been well documented, and student evaluation reports have consistently drawn attention to the generally sporadic nature of much of the student-tutor interaction, and the almost complete absence of opportunity for students to be in communication with each other. In addition, tutors have felt that although the majority of the unit materials were designed to be self-contained, many students had not worked consistently through them and had failed to complete the in-text exercises and activities. Opportunities to present outline and draft

assignments were also constrained by the slowness of surface mail, although a small number of students had access to fax machines.

The possibilities

Members of the programme team therefore wished to investigate ways of using modern communications technology in order to enhance the tutorial support given to students, provide opportunities for discussion with other students who were following the same units, and also allow tutors more effectively to help students pace themselves through the printed materials.

It was essential that the system selected should be accessible to non-computer specialists and should be based on a readily-available domestic technology. Videoconferencing was discounted at an early stage, and the University's e-mail systems were considered to be not all that user-friendly, were expensive of on-line time, and could not be used for conferencing. It was judged that Lotus Notes groupware would most effectively provide the facilities that were being sought. Like e-mail, Lotus Notes requires the University to set up a server (a central computer) through which all registered participants communicate.

The project

In March 1995 a successful application was made to the University's Enterprise in Higher Education (EHE) fund for three tutors to carry out a pilot project in computer-mediated communication (CMC) with a small sample of Certificate in Education distance students. All of the 250 students who were known at that time to be registering at the University centre in September were invited to apply to take part in the project, so long as they had access either at home or at work to the appropriate hardware (a telephone line, a computer capable of running Windows, and a modem).

The project ran until March 1996, and allowed for some two hours of preparation and staff development time per week for each of the tutors, the provision of software to the participants (about £60 each for the licence and the floppy disks), the services of the system manager, and facilities for carrying out an evaluation after the first semester of operation.

The software

Lotus Notes was designed primarily as a commercial groupware product to allow users to share information, data and files across a company network. It also provides for remote access via modems and the public telephone service. One of the advantages that it has over conventional e-mail is that its characteristic process of rapid 'replication' means that the on-line time is very short.

Lotus Notes allows a variety of communication modes: one-to-one (e-mail); conferencing with identified groups; conferencing with everyone in the system. Each database has a list of registered users, and can be accessed only by those who are authorised to do so. The facilities were used in the following ways:

One-to-one (e-mail) With students, e-mail fulfilled a tutorial function, and all the kinds of issues and queries habitually raised in tutorials took place here. Sometimes a student would try out a contribution on her tutor before placing it in the conference area for consideration by the rest of the group. Tutors also communicated with each other through e-mail, using the database primarily for electronic memos of an information-giving kind rather than for discussions.

Conferencing with identified groups   The conference areas used the particular features of Notes most effectively. Databases were opened for the following typical groups:

- the CMC project tutors;
- each tutor's tutor-group;
- students following each unit.

In the unit databases the tutor(s) would pose a question, raise an issue, or present a theme for discussion, and place it in the conference area; students would then respond to the question or to the responses of others.

Conferencing with everyone in the system   The general social area for everybody registered as a Notes user (including those participating in another pilot project) was called 'Cafe', and was intended as a recreational area for the discussion of any issue that anyone, student or tutor, wished to raise.

The tutors

It was important that if the project was to succeed it had to work with tutors who were not particularly expert in IT. The project leader, who had recently carried out a feasibility study in the use of CMC with adult distance learners, was the only computing specialist. He took on a considerable responsibility for training and supporting the other two, who were selected as experienced Certificate in Education tutors with an interest in exploring ways of improving communication with and between distance learners. Two tutors are full-time members of the University staff, who had computing equipment both at home and at work. The third member of the team is a part-time teacher in an FE college and a visiting tutor at Greenwich, with access to Notes only at home.

It did seem to be an advantage to have the possibility of access all through the week and around the clock, as tutors were often able to log on and deal with some of the accumulated correspondence when they had ten or fifteen minutes to spare from other activities, whether weekday teaching or weekend gardening. This made it very difficult to calculate exactly how much time tutors were spending on project work, and it also at times led to the feeling that they were never having a break from it.

For each tutor the project was timetabled to take up approximately one quarter of their scheduled teaching load for the semester.

The students

The participants were all involved in the teaching or training of others, and were anxious to try out this new method of providing tutorial guidance at a distance and encouraging peer support. None of them was a computing specialist.

The table gives details of the number (15F, 16M) involved in the project:

	Registered	Withdrew	Completed
Level 1	15	8	7
Level 2	16	3	13
TOTALS	31	11	20

At the end of Semester 1 a questionnaire was sent to all of the 31 students who had initially registered as participants. The results of this are presented below, together with the comments of the three tutors.

The feedback

Students' experiences:

Most of those who withdrew did so for the familiar reasons of ill-health or pressure of work; only two suffered unresolvable problems in acquiring equipment or installing the software. While telephone support was given by the system administrator to those with operational difficulties, it was not possible to offer visits to private homes in order to check malfunctioning equipment. A number of students were able to call on computer expertise at their places of work when they were in trouble.

By and large, student expectations of greater contact with tutors and with fellow-students were met, although they were not asked to articulate what their expectations were until after they had worked with Notes. The ability to receive or send messages at any time of the day or night without imposing one's own anti-social study habits on others was seen as a great benefit in reducing the feelings of isolation that are inevitably experienced by all distance learners. From the 'time of composition' which is displayed on all database entries it was clear that there were a fair number of late-night and early-morning workers among both tutors and students.

The e-mail 'tutorial' database was used consistently by learners to seek clarification of themes and issues from the unit materials, to help meet learning outcomes and prepare for assignments, to receive advice on administrative and procedural matters, and for general reassurance and guidance. Two students who had experienced great problems said that without support through CMC they would have had to withdraw totally from the programme. Students reported that they were well satisfied with the nature and quality of their interaction with tutors, and that they preferred communicating through Notes to making telephone calls or writing letters, largely because of its ease of use, its immediacy and its non-intrusiveness.

However, there were mixed responses to the many-to-many conference databases. It was generally felt that the competence-based and reflective units – which required the compilation of portfolios rather than the production of essay-type assignments – were less suitable for discussion between learners than the other more overtly content-based and discursive units. The presence of printed distance-learning support materials to guide an individual student in the preparation and production of evidence for a portfolio led to a need for consultation with the tutor rather than for a debate with peers.

Those unit materials which presented structured information and included clear in-text activities were particularly well suited to mediation through the conferencing facility. But there was a suggestion that women students were less likely to make lengthy contributions than men, and were more likely to feel inhibited in responding to the contributions of others. Some concern was also shown about the public nature of the electronic conferences where, unlike classroom seminars, contributions to a debate are 'archived'. Several students from the police and the armed services believed that they were sometimes a little less frank in their electronic comments than they might have been in a live discussion.

The 'Cafe' facility was little-used by the Cert Ed students, and those who did venture into it expressed surprise at the presence of participants from another pilot project. In the end, tutors put forward the idea of an alternative 'tutor-free' database to provide an arena for student socialising, but again little interest was shown in this proposal. (It is worth noting that course members such as these, whose prime institutional allegiance will be to their own college, show very little interest in general student affairs at the University of Greenwich.)

There were few serious problems with students' handling of the technology, although a two-week interruption in the operation of the University's server towards the end of the pilot project caused some frustration to both students and tutors. It did, though, produce a number of touching 'We missed you' messages, and it was interesting to observe that there were many students who had got so used to communicating with their tutors through Notes that they preferred to wait for it to be restored rather than pick up the telephone to make contact.

The key to effective use was the production and distribution of a clear *'Installation and First Steps'* guidance manual (written and designed by the IT-expert tutor in order to make it possible for participants quickly to become self-reliant) and the insistence that users should themselves carry out the software installation (a process involving 18 floppy disks). Some of the students found it difficult to read the lengthier on-screen documents, and used the facility to down-load and print the pages that they required. Two participants were a little ahead of the available technology in their hope to be able to mail assignments electronically and to access on-line reference materials and library catalogues.

Those who met face-to-face on the study day much enjoyed the opportunity for interaction with the fellow-students whose contributions they had been reading and responding to over the previous two or three months. Over lunch, one woman was heard to say to another, with an expression of astonishment: 'But I had assumed that you were a man!'.

Tutors' experiences:

It was very strongly felt that insufficient time had been allowed for the training and familiarisation of the two 'non-IT' tutors; almost half of the e-mail messages between tutors were concerned with operational issues in the use of Notes. It was fortunate that the students were very understanding of any difficulties that were being experienced, and were unfailingly good-humoured.

The process of tutoring itself was found to be more time-consuming than communicating with students either face-to-face or on the telephone. Tutors estimated that the time they spent on project-related activities well exceeded the amount of time allocated to them. The flexibility that CMC offered meant that it was often quite difficult – literally – to switch off from the tutoring activities. However, it was anticipated that the experience gained during the semester in operating the system and establishing procedures would enable the tutors to be more efficient in the future, and give them confidence in sharing their experience with new participants.

As tutors became more familiar with the students' way of approaching the use of Notes, they accepted that conferencing activities in particular needed to be structured and directed, as the students seemed to be less independent and autonomous than had been anticipated. In general, basic considerations regarding the conduct of classroom seminar discussions were still found to apply: tutors should acknowledge every student's contribution to the debate, should draw out the tentative and control the garrulous, should help structure and focus the issues under consideration, and should encourage students to interact with each other.

Towards the end of the semester, as assessment deadlines approached, students became increasingly instrumental in their use of tutors. There was less requirement for initiation of discussion, and more call for guidance on draft assignments.

By and large, tutors felt that the quality of their interaction with the active students was not diminished by the use of CMC, and that this mode of communication allowed the individual personality characteristics of both tutors and students to be evidenced in the electronic interchanges.

The conclusions

The pilot project has demonstrated that the use of CMC can contribute to the resolution of some of the problems experienced by adult distance students. It has enabled them to share ideas, experiences and opinions in a flexible way, free from the constraints of time and geography. It can reduce the feelings of isolation often experienced by such learners, and increase opportunities for access to and communication with both tutors and peers. It has allowed tutors to monitor students as they progress through the unit materials, and to receive and comment on drafts of work-in-progress.

The Lotus Notes software chosen for this project is complex, but proved to be friendly enough for someone familiar with the operation of Windows to be able to learn to use it relatively quickly and successfully. Students noticed little increase in their telephone bills, even when they lived some distance from London. However, participants did need to have access to a reasonably powerful, modern computer, preferably at home.

In order to give the confidence in the technology that can allow proper curriculum activity to be established and maintained, it is necessary to have reliable technical support continuously available to help both staff and students resolve problems as they arise. In addition, tutors need to have the opportunity to undertake appropriate staff development before working with students, and so have prior experience of the conferencing and e-mail environment. All users have to be as comfortable with the computer technology as they are with the pen and the telephone.

Using CMC impacts on the nature of distance education by: changing the relationship between students and tutors, facilitating peer tutoring and collaboration in a 'virtual' classroom, allowing colleagues to plan and carry out team teaching at a distance, altering the pace and structure of curriculum delivery, making the curriculum more accessible and student-centred.

It was found that regular and frequent connection to the system was desirable, in order to maintain momentum, interest and interaction. One student who had had to miss several weeks through illness reported on the difficulty of getting back into the system and coping with the daunting backlog of contributions to the conference databases. The other side of this, of course, is that the discussions had been archived, and so were still available to the student to be used as a resource. Another student, who in the end had not been able to install Notes, was able to come into the University on two occasions and read through all the relevant discussions that had taken place for each of the units she was taking.

So, CMC should not be seen as second-best to face-to-face teaching, but as a different kind of communication event, which can be linked to the provision of instructional materials at a distance. All participants get the chance to think about and reflect on issues and refer to other sources of information before either posing or responding to questions. Activities need to be well structured, though, with clear outcomes and deadlines, and it is best if following each period of conference discussion there is appropriate tutor or student summing-up before moving on.

The next steps
On the basis of what they have learnt from carrying out this project, the tutors are recommending that the scheme should continue to be offered to Cert Ed students, and extended to students following the BA Education & Training course, as distance learning materials become available at CATS level 3.

The high drop-out rate at level 1 was worrying, and steps will be taken to try out the competence-based and reflective units entirely on-line, without the support of printed materials. This could simulate the teaching model more realistically, and more clearly define the role of the personal tutor, unencumbered by the presence of the author of the printed materials.

It seems important that the induction and initial installation/connection processes are carried out rapidly, so that students become active participants as early in the programme as possible. Once this connection has taken place, consistent procedures for the monitoring and support of students will help to maintain their engagement with the scheme.

The tutors' own growing awareness of the wide range of facilities offered by Lotus Notes has led them to the conclusion that it should be exploited further as a curriculum and administrative support tool both within and beyond the School.

The electronic dispatch of all course materials and receipt of assignments seems to be a little further in the future, held back more by administrative and academic constraints than technical or operational ones.

Chapter Eleven

Towards World Wide Web courseware for the humanities: The problems of text on screen

Sarah Porter and Peter Childs

This is a case study about two strands of an on-going courseware development project within the School of Media, Critical, and Creative Arts (MCCA) at John Moores University, Liverpool. In 1993 the project was founded to investigate the possibility of presenting learning materials for undergraduates over the University's computer network. It was felt that, since the Section has a long history of providing students on all modules with paper handbooks, these could be supplemented by on-line materials.

Objectives

The challenges the project has had to face, and which will be touched upon in this case study, are as follows: presenting large sections of text on screen; meeting student resistance to information technology (hereafter IT); promoting an awareness of IT among academic and support staff; maintaining a sharp pedagogic focus and encouraging computer-based learning while avoiding the pitfalls of 'edutainment'. As well as explaining the work we have been engaged in, the case study aims to outline these problems and summarise the lessons learned by the different participants in the project: academic staff, computer support department, students, Learning Services (library personnel), and the Learning Methods (Open Learning) division of the university.

Below we will discuss the two strands of our overall project.

The Windows Help system

Our first venture was to provide learning materials for an introductory module in American Studies. This was a single semester, 15-week module, taught to approximately 100 first-year undergraduate students. Materials were developed to run in a Windows environment and the system was piloted in 1994. The on-line package included module details and background, lecture summaries, documents for seminars, open learning materials, and reading lists. An evaluation of the students' experience was conducted by a member of the University's Business School and results were circulated in early 1995.

The system was developed as a series of interlinked scrollable Windows Help-screens, divided into 16 sections, which provided week-by-week information (including lecture notes, seminar questions, primary source documents, and bibliographies). The Windows Help system was chosen because Windows is the University's standard operating system and we thought that anyone familiar with Windows would have no difficulty in using our package. An eight-page support document explaining the system was distributed to all students. Our Windows Help system was developed using a commercial package called 'Robohelp' and took a member of academic staff (supported by the University's Learning Methods department) about three months to develop, working on it for several hours each week. Materials were both typed and scanned in. When compiled, the system, which contained 12 bitmapped pictures and the equivalent to 120 pages of text, came to 1.2 megabytes (Mb) and was therefore able to be supplied to students on one high-density floppy disk as well as over the network.

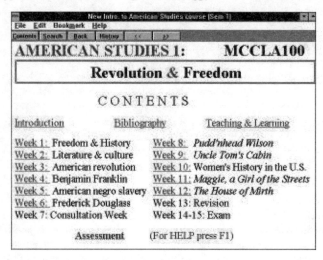

Fig. 1: Screen-shot of the Introduction to American Studies entry-level point

Student responses

The results of the module evaluation showed us that the institution, which offered much documentation but little actual induction, was over-estimating students' familiarity with computers. Even in 1994, only 15 per cent of our Humanities undergraduates felt that they had had any significant previous experience with IT. Many students require thorough education in operating a mouse and keyboard, and in computer software basics concerning, for example, file management and Windows. Another problem related to this, is cultural. While training combats issues of knowledge, a few students are still against the very idea of using computers, which are seen as 'toys', or 'uncreative', or axiomatically inferior to learning from a book. Solving this difficulty requires time and patience: a shift in social perceptions will be necessary. The problem is compounded by scepticism about the value of information technology among some members of academic staff and Learning Services. The benefits of paper-copy in terms of portability, familiarity, and ownership are repeatedly stressed above the benefits of IT approaches in terms of searchability, updatability, and cost. Access to computers is another fundamental issue. While our institution has a generous ratio of full-time students to computers of a little over 12:1, students complained that terminals were often unavailable. Having said all this, we should stress that the majority of students were happy using the Help system itself, once problems of training and availability had been overcome.

Following on from the trial (which has now run for three semesters), we decided to further develop the project in two directions during 1995. These addressed some of the difficulties encountered by the pilot system by, firstly, providing over the World

Wide Web (WWW) copyrighted materials which had previously been subject to limited access for students (too few books); and secondly, by presenting specialist materials in an interactive multimedia format (fragile, primary documents which had restricted access). The first system 'On-demand publishing in the humanities' is outlined below. 'Text, theory, event' will be outlined in Lisa McRory's case study, also in this book.

On-demand publishing in the humanities project: Objectives

For modules in the Humanities, the provision of sufficient key reading materials is a major difficulty as student numbers grow but funding does not. Building upon the work already completed within the School, the On-Demand Publishing project attempts to explore one solution to this problem. The project operates on two levels: first, in delivering carefully-selected, module-specific materials to students, via the university network; second, in exploring issues that are relevant in the wider context of electronic information delivery. These issues include: copyright; the problem of text on screen; digitisation of text; security of copyright information; staff and student responses. In this section of the case study, we offer an overview of the system and outline a number of issues and challenges the 'On-Demand Publishing' project has faced.

Project development

Due to the developmental work that had already been done within the School for the American Studies modules, we were fortunate in winning an award from the Electronic Libraries Programme, funded by HEFCE, within the 'On-Demand Publishing' section of the Programme. This funding allows two members of staff to devote 12 months to the development of complementary learning materials for three modules. We are also able to call upon the expertise of the University's Learning Methods Unit and the Computer Services Department. The Learning Services Department shares in the management of the project. Because the project uses copyright materials, external partners have been of major importance, and we are working closely with Routledge and Blackwell publishers to gain permissions and to explore payment mechanisms.

The materials are stored on and accessed from the main University WWW server. They can then be retrieved from any networked machine within the University by using a standard WWW Browser, Netscape. The choice of software was based upon the wish to create an easily replicable model; any institution which already runs a WWW server would be able to adopt the model. Furthermore, the WWW has already been established as something of a standard for the dissemination of information in electronic format, which has added value for the transferability of the project as a model.

At the time of writing, we are running the first of the three modules. 'Postmodernism and Fiction' is a third-year module, studied this year by 30 students. The on-line support material for the module provides key essays or extracts with hypertext links providing relevant cross-over points between the sections. The 25 articles range from fifteen to sixty pages in length in their original format, giving approximately 750 pages in total. In addition, a further eight custom-written two-page articles, which make up a thematic overview for the module, plus a summary of each of the copyright texts, have been produced by the member of staff responsible for the module.

The other two modules (one drawn from each of the Cultural Studies and American Studies subject areas) are designed with some variations in content and structure, in order to reflect the requirements of each module as it is taught. Each of

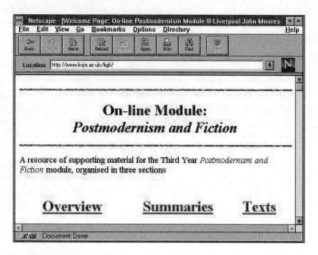

Fig. 2: Screenshot of the WWW 'Postmodernism and Fiction' module, entry point.

the three modules is also aimed at a different year-group. The WWW software allows students to use the materials in a number of ways: read the materials on screen, print them out (using the university network system), carry out key-word searches, or use a combination of these options. A point to make here is that the project is not intended to replace paper-based resources. We recognise that many students will wish simply to print materials but hope that the fact that they can browse through a larger body of data will encourage them to be selective in what they choose to print.

In terms of development, the module evolved through three main phases. Firstly, the materials that were to be used were selected or written by academic staff. Secondly, the materials were put into a standard digital text format. For the custom-written materials, this was a quick process – the materials had been produced in a word-processing package, so were simply re-saved as plain text. For the copyright extracts, the hard-copy versions had to be put through a digitisation process (see below) and saved as plain text. Thirdly, each digital version was 'marked-up' into the standard WWW-compatible format, Hypertext Mark-Up Language (HTML). These HTML tags dictate the layout of each document, the presence of any images, and the hyperlinks between the various documents.

From this stage, the documents could be transferred onto the University Server. The in-house materials are freely accessible to users both within the LJMU network and externally, via the Internet; the copyright materials are protected by two levels of security, so that they can only ever be accessed from within the university network, by users who have been allocated a specific username and password combination.

Issues

Having given an outline of the system, we will now sketch some of the key challenges involved in the project, and explore some of the issues that would have to be faced by anyone intending to take a similar approach.

Firstly, neither of the publishers with whom we are working have been able to supply us with digital versions of the majority of the key texts; therefore, with their permission, we have reproduced each page of the materials in a digital format. The creation of a digital page-image (from a standard, 'clean' published text with a common typeface) is a fast, straightforward process. Using a Hewlett Packard flatbed scanner, a digital version of a page of ordinary text can be produced in as little as thirty seconds. This image is essentially a digital photocopy of the entire page, and, because the blank space on the page is also saved with the text, it takes up a large amount of memory (about 1Mb per page). Although images can be viewed using WWW software, its usage is limited: it is not possible to carry out key-word searches on the text, or to include hyperlinks, and the large size of files causes problems for downloading and printing. The conversion of these images into plain text versions allowed us to implement these facilities. To do this we had to use Optical Character Recognition (OCR) software. OCR packages convert a digital image of text into a plain text equivalent. The current specifications of software of this type produce final copy that is approximately 95–99 per cent accurate, a figure which seems reassuringly high, until the implications of the 1–5 per cent inaccuracies are considered (that is, between one and five words in every hundred are inaccurate). In a project such as this, where the co-operation with publishers is only assured on the basis that their original text is faithfully reproduced, any inaccuracies cannot be tolerated. The only solution, therefore, is for each text to be put through a meticulous proof-reading and amendment process. This process is time-consuming: the scanning, OCR-ing, proof-reading and amending of each page of text takes between 30 minutes and an hour. OCR-ing does not, therefore, present a quick and easy solution to the problem of digitising text.

Secondly, an emphasis upon large quantities of text on-screen frequently presents difficulties for users, and this was acutely important to us since we were seeking to create a reading environment that was as 'user-friendly' as possible. Factors such as background colour and font-size play a crucial part in the creation of such an environment. With plain-text versions of the texts, we were able to use the functionality of HTML to specify an interface that was conducive to the use of text on screen. A pale background colour and dark type were selected as they rendered text clear and easy to read both on-screen and when printed. Font-size was left as the standard for WWW applications, which allows a user to specify a different font size from within the software if they wish. Maintaining the integrity of the original version of the text was a prerequisite of the project; however, this had to be balanced with the very different qualities that hard-copy and digital text present. Locating one's place within a book is intuitive; a different situation occurs when dealing with digital text. Whilst hyperlinks are valuable in allowing a user to move quickly between different documents, their use needs to be carefully considered if they are not to cause confusion. We attempted to counter this problem by providing a system of hyperlinks which direct the user back to central 'index' pages, which in turn present links to the other elements of the resource. However, no matter what structure is imposed when presenting text on screen, there can be no doubt that the navigation of such systems presents problems for many users.

Thirdly, the participation in the project of the two publishers, Routledge and Blackwell, has greatly facilitated the procedure of copyright clearance. They are both major publishers in the subject areas covered by 'Postmodernism and Fiction'; we could therefore rely wholly upon works for which they had rights when selecting the on-line texts. This situation will not apply to the other two modules; individual publishers and authors will have to each be contacted, as the central Copyright Licensing Agency does not deal with permissions for making use of texts in digital format. This situation greatly adds to requirements for staff time. Our relationship with the publishers has also been key in the establishment of payment mechanisms. A number of models for compensation have been suggested but agreement has been reached on the basis of a payment per page of text digitised and the number of users, rather than on actual usage of the texts. This model of payment would have serious implications for the expansion of the resource to include more modules containing copyright materials, as the costs incurred would be punitive and could not be realistically met in the long-term.

Student and tutor responses

The undergraduates following 'Postmodernism and Fiction' are in their third year, but formal IT training, at entry level, has only become a standard within the School in the last year (we intend to compare the responses of this untrained cohort with those of first-year students on a different module). The disadvantage which this lack of training brings to bear upon initiatives of this sort became clearly apparent at a hands-on training session organised to introduce the students to the on-line materials. Of the 21 students who attended the session, only four had previously made use of the university computer network and none had previously used a World Wide Web browser. Before the students could be introduced to the materials, we had to overcome the far more fundamental problems of introducing them to the basics of operating a computer. Despite these difficulties, most of the students had accessed the resource within the one-hour session.

The students' responses to the medium used was positive in the main; most seemed eager to equip themselves with IT skills and saw the limited introduction that they were receiving as a step towards achieving this. In general, staff responses were also positive. Once an initial unfamiliarity with the media had been overcome, the member of staff responsible for the module became a constant source of information, reporting on feedback that the students gave to him and attempting to define his requirements as precisely as possible. He also emphasised the most positive aspect of the provision of supporting materials in this way, from his point of view: that students could be confidently directed towards readings which were always available.

Implications for educators

The platform-independence and relative simplicity of Hypertext Mark-Up Language provides an accessible choice for the novice courseware author, with the distributed access afforded by the WWW as an added incentive. However, whilst the use of internally-produced digital materials presents few logistic problems in the development of on-line resources, the inclusion of copyright materials raises issues of obtaining rights, establishing payment mechanisms and the digitisation of source materials.

Issues around the integrity of the text, the fairness of supplying materials only in electronic format, plus the cost, speed, and portability of Internet documents, will continue to hold back electronic publishing in Higher Education. IT training and support for both staff and students need to be a primary consideration; as was discovered with both stages of the project, it plays a crucial role in the uptake of any computer-based initiative. Considerable hardware investment is also essential if IT is to be used effectively. However, as student numbers increase, technology becomes more widely available and understood, and modes of delivery diversify, the 'electronic book' will hold increasing prominence. On the one hand, we are aware that a number of problems remain with our system and with the way it is used by students – it is probably too early to expect humanities students, for many of whom computers are still intimidating, to interact with on-line systems to their best advantage. On the other hand, to maximise the benefits (and minimise the difficulties) that will accrue in the future, when students will almost certainly download lecture notes from the WWW, will have on-line seminars and access to huge virtual libraries, we need to start examining the possibilities of using the Internet for educational purposes now.

More details about the On-Demand Publishing project are available on the WWW at: **http://www.livjm.ac.uk/on_demand/**

Information about the other initiatives within the Electronic Libraries programme is available at: **http://ukoln.bath.ac.uk/elib/**

Chapter Twelve

Building learning webs

Martin Buck

Camosun College in Victoria, British Columbia, Canada is using telematics to create instructional systems that support the learning needs of Adult Basic Education (ABE) students. The goal of the project is to develop a Hypertext Markup Language (HTML)-based instructional system that will help ABE faculty facilitate individualised learning and allow instructors to customise instructional modules to accommodate individual students' diverse learning needs. Recent studies on the needs of developmental education's adult learners highlight the necessity for more flexible scheduling and increased access to academic, career and vocational upgrading opportunities. To meet this demand Camosun's ABE department established an ABE Open Lab at the Interurban Campus in October of 1995. The Learning Webs phase of the project focuses on the development of hypermedia based instructional modules to further expand flexibility of access and delivery of instruction. Implementation began in March 1996 with a training program for ABE faculty and staff which has provided them with hypermedia skills to create new curricula and convert existing materials to an electronic format. The English and math curricula modules are currently (May 1996) under development by Camosun faculty. These will be piloted in the Open Lab in the fall 1996 term. Adult learners in need of academic or vocational upgrading will be able to interact with ABE instructors and instructional modules from any location with a college network or Internet connection.

The context

In March 1995 the British Columbia Student Outcomes Steering Committee completed a report on the effectiveness of Adult Basic Education (ABE) programmes in provincial colleges. One of the major findings of the James report was the adult student's requirement for more flexible course scheduling and delivery. Camosun College in Victoria has long provided flexibility in its ABE offerings through continuous intake, individualised instruction and year-round programming. However, until Autumn 1995 classroom instruction continued to be offered only at set times and in few locations.

The demand for increased flexibility has always been clear to ABE faculty and staff. ABE students have been anything but 'traditional' students. Many come to Camosun's ABE programme with a set of challenges that few high school youth graduates face. Many adult learners are supporting single-parent families. A number are dealing with addiction issues. Low self-esteem due to unemployment, and more recently under-employment, is also an issue. The list of barriers to education faced by these mature learners is long. The James report discovered that due to these obstacles the majority of ABE learners take at least five years to complete their upgrading programme.

The college's projected financial situation dictated that the project had to be completed within a diminishing resource allocation framework due to a series of federal cuts to post-secondary education. Camosun's President (Ashton 1995) estimated that the next three years would see cross-college budget reductions of up to ten per cent per year. Camosun's ABE programme, like most college ABE programmes, is driven by FTEs, or full time equivalencies. Every month a count of student numbers is taken. If classrooms are less than full, the following year the programme may lose an FTE, that is a faculty or staff member may lose their position. The result is a corresponding decrease in the number of classes the ABE department is able to offer. A major goal of the Learning Webs project is to develop appropriate technologies and systems that will allow faculty and staff to effectively increase services to students. The business world has already demonstrated how the application of information technology can increase effectiveness. The appropriate use of these same technologies in the service of students, combined with useful data management systems, should provide similar gains in efficiency for ABE programmes.

Objectives of the project

Phase One of the Open Access Lab

In 1993, to meet the demands for greater and more cost-effective access to Camosun College's Adult Basic Education programmes, the department initiated planning for the Open Access Lab. In October 1995, using existing conventional instructional resources, the first phase of the Open Lab began accepting new students. The new lab provides daily, sometimes even hourly, intake to an ABE programme that offers the flexible course scheduling and delivery called for in the James report. Adult learners wishing to enter Camosun who do not have the necessary prerequisites, including those who have been out of high school for more than three years, complete a maths and English assessment. Adult learners who require upgrading are then granted immediate entry to Camosun's ABE Open Lab. The lab offers English and maths upgrading instruction to complete the prerequisites for trades, technology, university transfer and college diploma programmes. While ABE instruction at Camosun has always been individualised and self-paced, instruction was offered only in traditional classrooms at set inflexible times. The first phase of the lab, using existing resources, offers more flexible course scheduling. Faculty and staff are available from 8.30am to 8.00pm Monday to Friday, with the exception of Tuesday when the lab closes at 3.30pm and Friday when it closes at 12 noon. This model has allowed Camosun's ABE department to increase student access by 27 per cent. Thanks to the Lab's innovative use of existing resources as well as faculty-developed print modules, adult learners receive the upgrading they need at times that meet their schedule.

Phase Two: Electronic delivery of instruction

The telematics phases of the ABE Open Lab focus on providing the faculty with the resources necessary to expand electronically the efficiency and effectiveness of the Open Lab. This expansion includes the development of hypermedia instructional offerings to current ABE students as well as other Camosun students in the midst of their programmes who discover upgrading needs. Faculty-developed instructional modules using a variety of media, delivered via the college's computer network, will allow ABE to expand its services to students in other departments. These modules are being developed using the hypertext markup language (HTML). HTML products like

Microsoft's *Internet Assistant for Windows* allow instructors to take existing word-processed print modules and convert them into the HTML format. This electronic hypermedia form includes provision for electronic print, graphics, video and audio. Camosun faculty's annual two months of development time has been leveraged by an innovations grant from the college. The grant has provided the hardware, software, training and support resources necessary to complete this phase of the project. The goal of this phase of the project is to provide the faculty with the expertise necessary to develop hypermedia modules and achieve further efficiencies in the existing Open Lab. The piloting of the first of these modules takes place in September 1996.

Phase Three: Delivery of instruction to other campuses

The next phase, scheduled for completion in September 1997, will see the electronic delivery of these hypermedia instructional modules. The department's intent is to make these resources available to any college student in any programme on any campus who needs remedial or upgrading assistance. Phase Three will begin with delivery to the ABE computer lab at the Lansdowne campus. Thanks to the college's inter-campus computer network as well as the network-friendly capabilities of HTML, further increase in student FTE is expected. Any college network-connected computer, including the general purpose computer labs, will be able to receive and display ABE instructional modules. Thus learning webs will be created between ABE faculty and virtually any college student who discovers upgrading needs in the midst of their career programme. The network transmission capabilities of these modules will eventually permit the ABE department to offer just-in-time instruction to workers off-campus at their job site or community action group.

Phase Four: Delivery of instruction to the work site

This phase of the Learning Webs project has the ABE department offering community or work site-based instruction using telematics by September 1997. Learners needing skill upgrading, both former Camosun students and those who have never darkened the college corridors, will have access to ABE faculty expertise. This phase will tie in well with the college plans to decentralise its community education programmes. Under this plan, currently being implemented, each college division is assigned three programmers, one from community education, one from international education and one from co-op education. These individuals, along with faculty representatives and the division dean, will comprise a Management Segment Team. Their principal task will be to develop courseware offerings for delivery both within and beyond the college's traditional territory of southern Vancouver Island. This task ties in well with the Learning Webs project's ultimate goal of establishing a delivery paradigm outside the 'bricks and mortar' of the existing infrastructure, using the college's Internet connections.

Phase Five: Delivery of instruction over the Internet

By 1998 the total number of people connected by the Internet is expected to reach 125 million worldwide. Phase five of the Learning Webs project uses telematics to expand delivery of ABE course offerings via the college's Internet connections. As more and more homes and offices become equipped with Internet-connected computers, Camosun instructors will be able to extend their influence well beyond Camosun's two campuses and offer the ultimate in flexible course scheduling and delivery.

Table 1. Five Phases of the Learning Web Project.

Phase	Location	Start Date
1	Interurban ABE Open Lab using existing delivery methods	October '95
2	electronic modules piloted at Interurban Open Access Lab	September '96
3	expansion to Lansdowne campus and any college-networked computer	September '97
4	work site-based delivery	September '98
5	Internet-based delivery	September '99

Summary: The Learning Web's aims and goals

All digital information sources, available at the speed of light over global networks, are converging on and available through the Internet at an exponential growth rate. There will be a corresponding demand for instructors who can structure the information glut that is the Internet into a form that makes sense to learners. This task is anything but new to instructors. Learners come to educational institutions because of the faculty's ability to structure information into forms useful to students. Most of the courses offered to students already exist in the printed form in libraries and other reference sources. Why don't more students involve themselves in a self-study programme? Perhaps it is because humans need a community. It is learning communities where this chaos called the information age can be ordered in ways that are useful and make sense to adult learners. Thus the goal of the Learning Webs project is to use telematics to create an instructional system that provides increased flexibility of course delivery and access to adult developmental education learners.

The programme: Beyond traditional course delivery

A hypermedia instructional delivery system

The hypermedia capabilities of the Internet's World Wide Web are key components for the telematics phase of the Open Lab. Hypermedia is a computer software programme that can help instructors create links between related pieces of information. Imagine a stack of cards, each with information on a specific subject. Attached to each card is a button. Each button connects the user to another information card containing an educational resource or information source. Imagine further that this resource is not limited to print or text. It could be an audio or video segment, or even an entire multimedia encyclopedia. Now connect this stack of information cards via a telecommunications network to millions of computers around the world. On each of these computers is a software programme that allows students to manipulate electronically this stack of cards. An archive of the sum of the world's knowledge in text, graphics, sound and video is all there at the click of a button . Now expand those local and global connections to include other interactions with students and teachers in any country in the world. This is the World Wide Web, which links learners to any information, person or place desired.

The emerging hypermedia capabilities of networked computers are already dramatically altering learning paradigms. The world's largest computer network, the Internet, connects educational, government and commercial institutions in over 35 countries. A World Wide Web document available from the British National Council for Educational Technology illustrates the power of the Internet.

> *It is the 21st century version of an 18th century French project born of the optimism of the Age of Enlightenment: to create a single encyclopaedia of everything known by mankind. The French were defeated by the sheer growth of information and by the lack of technology to store and access it. As we approach the 21st century, however, the Internet could be that encyclopaedia – and much more (*Highways for learning: An introduction to the Internet for schools and colleges, *1995: 3).*

Governments throughout the world have committed to link every school, college, institute and university in their region to this resource. The next task is to provide instructors with opportunities to develop hypermedia courseware skills. Instructors will then be able to use these links to apply more efficiently and effectively the amalgam of curriculum design that is encapsulated in andragogy.

Hypertext Markup Language

The hypertext markup language (HTML) is the software programme that allows for the relatively effortless electronic publishing of documents containing text, animation, graphics, video, and audio. Web or HTML electronic documents have become even easier to use and create thanks to some new, often free, products offered over the Internet. Now anyone who can read, create and manipulate word processed documents can, with those same skills, read, create and manipulate hypermedia Web documents. Reference was made earlier to a British National Council for Educational Technology (NCET) document titled *Highways for learning: An introduction to the Internet for schools and colleges*. This electronically published document, or Web page, was retrieved over the Internet from NCET's Web site. If this document had been electronically published on the Web, a mouse click on any of the above italicised words would connect the reader to the NCET Internet address where the electronic pages are kept and updated regularly. HTML also permits the electronic publishing of any multimedia event the author chooses. For example, in a Web-based document the reader could use the computer mouse to click on an icon or picture of a radio speaker. Providing the author has made the appropriate hyperlinks, the reader could then hear the author's voice played through the computer's sound card and speakers. As the Internet's capacity for carrying data increases, student Web users will also be able to video conference with their instructors interactively. Therefore the Web offers some intriguing possibilities for structuring information in an educationally sound manner.

Camosun's Learning Webs project is developing instructional modules using HTML's facility for integrating electronic print, graphics, video and audio over telecommunication networks. The modules can be created using an editor or word processor. An instructor who is able to manipulate a word processor has the basic skill set to create electronic hypermedia documents. Microsoft offers a series of free add-ons to their Office line of software products. These 'Internet Assistants for Windows' are available for the *MS-Word* word processor, the *MS-Excel* spreadsheet, the *MS-Powerpoint* presentation manager and the *MS-Access* database. Each of these makes the creation of an electronic Internet web document as easy as sending the same file to a printer. Thanks to these information technologies the ABE faculty, which has already proven to be adept at structuring information to meet individual learner needs, will see its influence extended and facilitated by the use of these information technologies.

To accomplish the task of Web page creation and manipulation, instructors have been provided with the appropriate hardware, software and most importantly training opportunities and technical support. An Internet trainer and consultant was hired to teach faculty and staff how to collaborate on the use and creation of hypermedia-based curriculum to further expand the efficiency and effectiveness of the Open Lab. This training included the use of the *Eudora* e-mail package, the *Netscape Navigator* web browser, and the HTML editors, Microsoft *Word for Windows' Internet Assistant* and Sausage Software's *Hot Dog Pro*. The goal of this phase of the project is to provide ABE instructors with the tools and skills to master the use and creation of World Wide Web hypermedia instructional modules and thus interact with students in a multi-modal fashion. Rather than limiting their contact with students to one location and one time, instructors will be electronically linked with students. This curriculum will be delivered in traditional as well as electronic formats, the latter over the college's network and eventually the Internet.

The results

The first few months

The Open Lab and its second phase, the Learning Webs project, have only been under way for a few months. Department members have received instructions in honing their Internet and HTML skills. They have developed pages for the department's Intranet or internal college computer network. These electronic pages have been created to tell students and other members of the college community about ABE department programmes. Faculty members have also identified existing print curriculum resources that they will convert to HTML format. These include the following:

- instructor-authored supplements to the existing maths textbooks
- a compendium of English students' writing
- maths tests
- a learning guide for adults returning to college
- an instructor's reading course complete with links to World Wide Web magazines, newspapers, and radio and television stations
- a course syllabus for the department's Basic Academic Skills Development programme

In the latter stages of the Learning Webs training programme, the faculty and staff from ABE's sister departments were invited to participate. Their HTML curriculum development projects include materials to meet Adult Special Education, Learning Skills and Basic Job Readiness Skills Training needs. As these adjuncts to regular programmes are being piloted, ABE maths and English curriculum committees are developing plans for the creation of complete online courses. Readers with an Internet connection can view the project results by directing their web browser to http://www.camosun.bc.ca/~abe.

Although the project is still in the early stages, some trends are worth noting.

The diversification and innovative use of instructional resources has allowed Camosun's ABE department to increase student access by 27 per cent. In response to this increased productivity of the Open Lab and the innovation efforts demonstrated by the Learning Webs team, the college administration waived a projected decrease in department funding. College administrators increased funding to the department. The extra funds have been used to hire a staff person to provide instructional assistance and computer technical support of existing and future phases of the project.

Faculty and student response

Eighty percent of the ABE department faculty and staff have taken part in at least one session of Learning Webs telematics training. By the end of May 1996, 20 per cent had completed their first home pages. It should be noted that due to limited resources, all of this training has taken place outside of the regular school day at times when the Open Lab's ten Internet capable workstations have been available to train faculty and staff. Faculty response to training has been very positive. Students have also been very supportive of the Open Lab. The steady increase in enrolment bears out the statement that they appreciate the flexibility and individualised instruction offered in the lab. While the first Learning Webs modules will not be delivered until September 1996, students are being introduced to the World Wide Web through the lab's Internet connected workstations. Student response is invariably one of great curiosity as well as a desire to learn about and become part of the World Wide Web electronic community.

There are, of course, dark patches to this silver cloud. Many faculty members at Camosun are this author's age and older (that is, they are over forty). Some researchers suggest that age can be a factor in a faculty member's decision to embrace new technology. The 20 per cent of faculty and staff members who chose not to take part in the Learning Webs training are mostly in the upper end of that category. That said, the two most enthusiastic adopters of this technology are both within a few years of retirement. Some faculty members feel threatened by the shift of focus from instructor at centre stage to instructor at the side facilitating and guiding students. Fortunately the imbedded andragogical culture of the ABE programme at Camosun has meant that these faculty members are in the minority.

Positive faculty and staff attitudes towards the ABE Open Lab project have been encouraged by efforts of the college's president, the dean of ABE's Access Division, and the chair of the faculty association negotiating committee. All three have acted as positive and effective change agents. In her first speech to the college community in 1994, the president spoke about the many people in the Camosun community who had expressed a wish to see the pace of change at the college lessen. Her response was that the only constant of the late twentieth century is change. To help develop an environment that encourages productive change, she has supported and encouraged innovation projects within the college and annual innovations conferences. At the college's annual innovations conferences, faculty and staff were provided opportunities to showcase projects and share ideas with their colleagues and selected members of the larger educational community. Shortly after his appointment, the dean of ABE's division presented the original vision for the Open Lab to the department. He instigated discussion on the benefits and logistics of an open lab and arranged funding for developmental work. A third source of positive attitudes towards the Open Lab project originates with the chair of the faculty negotiating committee. He and his committee successfully negotiated an advantageous faculty development commitment from the college. In exchange for several years without salary increases, each faculty member now has two months of time (in addition to holidays) to pursue professional, curriculum and institutional development activities. In an age where knowledge is doubling at an exponential rate, it is critical that faculty have the time to master new methods of curriculum delivery as well as the time to apply this new knowledge. The conscious change management of these college leaders, coupled with a climate of government cutbacks, has meant that most department members have been supportive of the Open Lab and the Learning Webs project.

Issues

Hardware and software

The department still lacks the resources to allow all faculty members, not to mention students, to become involved in the project. The site of the department's Open Lab, the trades and technology-focused Interurban campus, is very well networked. Most of the buildings have been constructed or updated with modern wiring in the last five years. Thus any faculty or staff member with a PC can be immediately connected to the college network and the Internet. The college's other campus, Lansdowne, with approximately the same student population, is much older and poorly networked. Only one departmental PC has a network connection at that campus.

Even the Interurban campus, as of late Spring 1996, does not have sufficient student workstations to properly pilot the modules being created. The Open Lab's ten network- capable machines are currently monopolised by English students who use them mostly for word-processing.

Fortunately software is becoming easier to obtain. As mentioned earlier, most of the products required to created and peruse HTML documents are available free or at a very nominal charge over the Net. Microsoft also supplies their Office product to educators at very reasonable prices. *MS-Office Pro*, which costs over $500 Canadian, is available for just over $100 Canadian when purchased as a license for 50 or more machines.

Technical support resources

A major problem has been obtaining access not only to the technology needed to create electronic learning webs, but also to the expertise in making the hardware and software work. The college's budgetary officers and computing services support staff are besieged with requests from faculty and students for Internet connections. Computing and telematics resources, formerly the sole prerogative of the computing technologists, are now being demanded by the ordinary college population. To meet this need, the ABE department has had to be rather creative. Once the first phase of the Open Lab was proven successful and the department demonstrated its willingness to pursue further innovations to increase productivity, the dean was able to persuade college officials to find allocate additional resources. An instructional assistant who also has skills as a computer technician has been hired full-time. This person provides hardware and software expertise as well as liaison between computing services and the department. With this resource in place, limited funds have been stretched by upgrading old castoff machines with new motherboards at a reduced cost over the price of a new machine.

Time

While faculty members have two months' annual leave to pursue professional, curriculum and organisation development, time to accomplish all of the project's goals is still an issue. To reach the September 1996 date for piloting the first of the modules, training began in early March, when most instructors had a full course load. Thus they were trying to master new tools for curriculum development at the same time as continuing with a full teaching assignment. Time constraints on support staff were also an issue. Their collective agreement allows for limited professional development activities. When time was found for them, they asked that the trainer focus on day-to-day immediate support issues that arose as they helped adult learners master basic word processing skills rather than HTML development skills.

Further development

While the instructional modules under development have yet to be piloted, a number of factors critical to the development of an effective telematics system have been identified. Learners need a system that helps them feel self-confident and self-reliant as they use this technology to achieve their educational goals. Adult Basic Education instructors want telematics-based instructional systems to meet sound andragogical principles and provide even greater facilitation of students' learning. They also want systems that will ease the clerical workload of testing, filing and the myriad other tasks required in the management of a classroom. Other stakeholders are looking for a technology that improves the faculty's ability to structure information in new media and markets, so that student access to college programmes increases. For all stakeholders, the most important issue is the ease with which the modules can be modified to meet ever-changing instructor and learner needs. The ultimate goal of this project is to develop electronic instructional modules that will help create a learning community where the 'world [is] made transparent by communications webs (Illich, 1971: 157).'

The goal of the Learning Webs project, implemented in the context of the growing sophistication of knowledge about instructional design for the adult learner, is to provide a flexible, innovative and multi-modal medium for instruction. Such an approach would extend the instructor's influence beyond the walls of the classroom to help create Illich's world made from transparent webs. Such a system would encourage choice and structure for both learner and instructor by offering modularisation of curriculum, self-pacing, and interactive feedback. Critical to all of this, however, is the provision by instructors of a structure to encourage the development of good research skills and work habits in students. Under such a system the instructor moves away from the role of information dispenser to that of learning facilitator and courseware developer.

As faculty's abilities to create electronic learning webs increases, the result will be instruction offered to adult learners in a time-and-space-independent fashion. Thus ABE faculty will also be able to offer instruction to adult learners who discover upgrading needs in the midst of their career or university transfer college programmes. Faculty prepared as well as appropriately modified 'off-the-Internet' hypermedia modules delivered through a variety of media will allow the ABE program to diversify its services to students well beyond the confines of the Open Lab.

Project progress reports from the delivery and piloting of the first hypermedia modules to the Open Access lab, will be posted on the Learning Webs home page at http://www.camosun.bc.ca/~abe. Later phases will see the use of telematics to expand the ABE programme students on other campuses and in other departments. The goal is to make resources available to any college student, in any programme, who needs remedial or upgrading assistance. This will be accomplished by expanding instructional delivery to other Camosun computer labs. Thanks to the college's inter-campus computer network, as well as the network-friendly capabilities of the HTML instructional modules, students will be able to interact with ABE instructors and curricula using any computer connected to the college network. These modules will also allow the department to leverage its resources to offer just-in-time instruction to workers at the job site. Thus ABE instruction can also be offered to workers at the job site with access provided via telephone, modem and office computer.

The project's ultimate goal is to establish an entrepreneurial delivery paradigm that stretches beyond the existing infrastructure, using the college's Internet connections. The end result of this project will be the offering of instruction to any adult learner who has a computer connected to the Internet. Thus instructors will be able to extend their influence well beyond Camosun's two campuses to anyone with an Internet connection, anywhere on the globe.

References

Ashton, E. (November 1994,) President's Performance Objectives. *Inside Camosun*, Victoria, BC: Camosun College.

B.C. ABE Student Outcomes Steering Committee. (March 31, 1995) *B.C. ABE Student Outcomes Report*. Vancouver, BC: Office of Institutional Research, Vancouver Community College

Highways for learning – An introduction to the Internet for schools and colleges. (1995). [World Wide Web Home Page]. (British) National Council for Educational Technology. Available at http://ncet.csv.warwick.ac.uk/WWW/randd/highways/index.html.

Illich, I. (1971). *Deschooling Society*. New York: Harper & Row

Notes

[1] The Internet address for this NCET quote is
http://ncet.csv.warwick.ac.uk/WWW/randd/highways/ch1.html.

[2] All of these software programs are available free of charge over the Internet from the respective publishers. Eudora is available at
http://www.qualcomm.com/ProdTech/quest/.Netscape Navigator is available from http://home.netscape.com/comprod/mirror/index.html. The Microsoft Internet porducts can be found at http://www.microsoft.com/internet. Hot Dog Pro is available from Sausage Software in Australia at http://www.sausage.com. There is a 30-day free trial version that can be upgraded to a registered version over the Net for a nominal amount.

Chapter Thirteen

Three Ws in nutrition:
Two universities working together

Betty Walsh

Australia is a vast country with an overwhelming majority of the population on certain sections of the coast, and a sparse population in the centre desert. The project described below involves two Australian universities, (one traditional, one non-traditional) on opposing sides of the continent. The two universities differ in their ethos, degree environment and course structure and in the emphasis of their courses.

The aim of the project was to enhance the teaching and learning process of veterinary students at both universities using a combination of technologies and student interaction. The technologies employed were the Internet (World Wide Web and e-mail) and compressed digital two-way video, two-way audio video conferencing. Funds for this project were obtained through a competitive process organised by the Committee for the Advancement of University Teaching. This is a national body with a remit to encourage improvements in teaching in the university sector.

Why would two universities become involved in a joint project?

Both schools of Veterinary Science were dissatisfied with the availability of materials for nutrition, particularly materials that showed the relationship between nutrition, preventative medicine, and the need to show the facts in the context of clinical problems and cases.

From the outset it was decided that the end product would be in an electronic form. The electronic form would give more flexibility and encourage the students to interact with the material. The World Wide Web was chosen as both schools would have ease of access to the materials. The World Wide Web also allows materials to be updated and expanded with relative ease. (Brown, 1995)

Two types of electronic communication were used: videoconferencing and e-mail. Videoconferencing allowed for realtime face-to-face communication, where as e-mail allowed for the students to participate in discussions at their leisure.

What was involved in the project?

During the project a set of World Wide Web documents on vitamins and minerals was developed. The documents included text, graphics, links to related web sites and suggested other resources (mainly books). The materials that were developed were used by third and fifth (final) year veterinary science students at both universities.

The content of the documents included basic general information about vitamins and minerals, basic information about individual vitamins and minerals, the biochemistry of vitamins and minerals both general and specific, diseases associated with vitamins and minerals (deficiency and toxicity), and the prevention and treatment of such diseases.

Statements and questions were given in the documents for students to ponder on, or think about. The purpose of these pondering points was to encourage the students to interact with the materials as well as provide topics to promote e-mail discussion amongst the students. For the students to use the technology effectively several small Internet training sessions were held. The sessions included the use of e-mail, Netscape and searching the Internet for information.

In October 1995 the final year students of both universities were involved in a series of video conferences. The content of these video conferences was based on the information in the World Wide Web resource and promoted interaction between the two sites.

For the students involved in the videoconferencing, information sessions on how to use the equipment and techniques that could be employed to enhance their communication with the other site were held. These sessions were held jointly for Murdoch University students and the University of Sydney students.

How did this project integrate into the total teaching process?

Four groups of students, two from each university, were involved in this project. The groups consisted of a group of third year students and a group of fifth (final) year students from each university.

For the third year students at Murdoch University their interaction with the materials took place during allocated tutorial times. The students were encouraged to use the resource and

e-mail at other times. The situation for the Sydney students was different. For interaction to occur between the students, the Sydney students participated in the course out of sequence with their timetable. The Sydney students were given credit for the course in the following semester, though it did increase their work load in the First Semester.

Final year students at Murdoch University enrolled in this project as one of their choices as an elective in their range of special topics. Final year students at the University of Sydney participated in this project as part of their clinical rotation.

What problems were encountered?

The problems that were encountered in this project can be divided into three categories; academic, instructional design and physical.

Academic problems

The problems encountered here included:

- differing teaching strategies of the two institutions involved;
- varied sequencing of educational materials;
- differing priorities of each faculty;
- the anticipated use of the materials by students at varying knowledge levels.

Overcoming these obstacles was not always possible. Careful negotiation was required to find solutions. If a solution to the problem could not be found, in most cases a compromise was made, for example the inclusion of material in the course materials that not all the content experts considered relevant.

The interaction between the students from the two universities was not as successful as was anticipated at the commencement of the project. The interaction was partly impeded by the physical restraints that are discussed under the heading *Physical*. The e-mail discussions were very slow even though suggested topics were included in the materials. In hindsight the students needed more initial guidance on the mechanics of e-mail and discussion lists, and how to participate in electronic discussions.

Instructional design

The problem here was to get the content experts to see the new course materials as a multi-level non-linear document in which there is no predetermined pathway. Though two of the content experts had attended formal training sessions on using the World Wide Web they still needed to gain a greater understanding of the technology. It was important that the content experts saw the unique nature of the technology being used and discovered ways of utilising its unique features in their course materials. This meant providing lots of examples of material.

Once the content experts had an idea of a multi-level non-linear document the instructional designer developed one small section of a document as template for the content experts where the style is only small pieces of information given at one time. The content experts then 'plugged' the required information into the document.

Also, to achieve the multi-level linking and to provide ease of flow, it was decided to use a common set of linking words throughout the documents. In reality this proved difficult though documents did use common linking words as much as possible.

Having students with varying knowledge levels also proved a challenge in the development of the resource materials. So that the less knowledgeable students were not overwhelmed by information that would possibly be difficult for them to understand, the content was presented in small chunks with links to more involved and complex information for those who wanted or needed more detail.

Physical

Initially there was inadequate availability of computer access to undergraduate students at both universities. This has greatly improved since the start of the project, and is continuing to improve. One faculty has installed a new student computer laboratory. Issues that have arisen from the installation of the laboratory are security and undergraduate access to the Internet.

The issue of access was considered in the application for the grant. It was thought both faculties would have improved and suitable student access in time for this project. For varying reasons this was not the case and a less-than-satisfactory plan was implemented.

Words of caution

For this type of resource to be used effectively the needs that are being addressed must be *real* rather than *perceived* needs to use the technology. The technology must be the appropriate vehicle for presenting the material. If this is not the case, the materials will become just another set of course resources that *sit on a shelf*.

Another caution is to avoid becoming too involved in the technology, particularly in the early stages of the project. Observations made during this project suggest that an emphasis on encouraging human interactions during the planning and development of an electronic resource should take priority over the technological aspects if student learning and faculty enjoyment are to be maximised.

What is the future of this project?

This project has the potential to be developed indefinitely but is dependent on the enthusiasm of staff and students. This potential exists because of the nature of the World Wide Web.

The resources are being used again this year with an emphasis on the students interacting with the materials. The resource is being enlarged with the aid of the students.

The discussion group or listserve has now been enlarged to include other veterinary science students. The discussions are now more general than about a specific course.

While the students responded positively to the technology, they also valued the stimulation of breaking the traditional isolation of Australian veterinary students by working with their peers from across the continent. Faculty found that the need for different specialists to collaborate catalysed the development of seamless integrated course materials and gave them insight into their teaching.

References
Alexander, Shirley. (1996) Seminar, Murdoch University, Western Australia.
Brown, Peter J., (1995) 'Creating educational hyperdocuments: can it be economic?',
   Innovations in Education and Training International, 32, 3, 202–208.
URL:http://numbat.murdoch.edu.au/nutrition/vits_min.html

Chapter Fourteen

Skills in creating networked information resources for teaching and learning

Geoff Rhen

This case study will give an overview of a project at Murdoch University that was (and is, given its ongoing nature) concerned explicitly with academic staff development in the area of the use of information resources for teaching and learning. The project was funded under the 1995 Academic Staff Development Fund, administered by the federal Department of Employment, Education and Training (DEET). Although the project requirements were that it be targeted towards academic staff, both general non-academic staff and the broader community (including those outside the University itself) could access the materials developed and, in the case of general staff on campus, attend face-to-face sessions.

All of the material referred to is online, via the Internet's World Wide Web, and a list of Uniform Resource Locators (URLs) is given at the end of the case study, for those who wish to pursue the documents further, using a Web browser such as Netscape or Mosaic.

Background

The following is an extract from the original submission to DEET:

'The context for this program is rapid growth in opportunities for networked information resources and network services to be used in teaching and learning, and the current absence of staff development measures to disseminate the new skills required to take advantage of these opportunities.'

Thus, it was intended that a structured programme of staff development be made available such that academic staff might acquire new skills in order to utilise more successfully information technology, in particular networked information resources, in their teaching and learning. In effect, this reduced to a programme both online and face-to-face, whereby staff acquired skill in writing HyperText Markup Language (HTML) for the development of documents for the Web.

Process of initial dissemination

One of the major challenges within an organisation can be ensuring the adequate dissemination of the availability of staff development courses to the targeted bodies. Murdoch University is fortunate in that there is an existing network of information technology (IT) contacts, part of whose role is to inform colleagues within their various departments and schools. These contacts are all subscribed to an e-mail list. Thus, initial advice of the proposed course was posted to this IT contact list. A World Wide

Web page had been constructed that included a proposed draft syllabus as well as an online registration form. The initial e-mail to the IT contacts pointed off to this online resource, as well as including the draft syllabus and a registration form within the e-mail.

Part of the intent of this strategy was to provide some information on the existing skills base of those who expressed interest in the course. The proposed course was not to be concerned with how to access the Web or use other network information retrieval skills such as say File Transfer Protocol (FTP) but to write and publish for the Web, using the above-mentioned Hyper Text Markup Language (HTML). A not insignificant number chose to register by e-mail rather than the Web and a depressing very few printed a hardcopy of the e-mail and filled this out longhand.

The initial e-mail sought feedback on the proposed syllabus, to ensure it met users' needs, as will as asking what computer platform (Windows or Macintosh) they preferred, in addition to asking what would be their preferred method of delivery: intensive hands-on sessions of two hours per day over a non-teaching week, semester-long courses of a one-hour per week lecture-type presentation, or purely online access at their leisure. As expected, there were a wide variety of responses. Thus, it was decided to develop a series of online lessons that were rich in illustrative examples and self-testing exercises, that would serve as the basis for presentation as lecture content, self-paced learning in a hands-on workshop setting or as an online reference source for learners to study when desired. Feedback via formal evaluation indicated that this approach was well received by all client groups, meeting the needs of those who desired hands-on practice in a structured learning environment as well as those who would prefer to learn at their own pace, in their own environment.

Assumed skills

The course was designed to develop skills in developing resources for distribution via the Internet, with a prime emphasis on learning HTML. As such, it was not intended to instruct in the basic use of such network information retrieval skills as the use of FTP (File Transfer Protocol) to move files from one's desktop development platform to the Web server machine. Also, a reasonable assumption was made that course participants would be quite familiar and comfortable with their preferred platform and knew their way around the machine's operating system.

In my experience of the hands-on workshops, there was a clear distinction between the prior skill of those users who operated under the Windows PC environment and those whose primary platform was the Macintosh. No attempt is made to explain this difference in this particular case other than to say that the PC users tended to be those whose work was more directly involved with the use of Information Technology, whereas the Macintosh users tended to be drawn from a broader base. The upshot was that time in the Macintosh hands-on sessions was spent instructing in what I would call reasonably basic skills before the prime purpose of a particular instruction session could be met. Thus, I would be inclined in future to perhaps screen participants beforehand, or offer a short course in preparatory skills.

Content

The course was concerned with developing skills in preparing documents for publication on the Internet via the World Wide Web. Participants could choose the level of skills to which they wished to aspire, and had the freedom to 'drop out' of the course as their needs were met. Such skills as creating interactive online fill-out forms are relatively sophisticated and were of no interest to some, at least at the commencement of the course. Others desired to acquire as many skills as possible.

Many academics desired simply to be able to take their existing course material, which might exist in word processed electronic format, and 'mark up' that material so that it would be accessible on the Web. Others were more ambitious in that they wished to create 'Web sites' that reflected their research interests and perhaps included graphics, as well as online forms for feedback. Whatever the need, the course was designed to be able to provide skills ranging from the basic to the quite sophisticated. Being online meant that lessons would form a reference resource that could be accessed as needed.

A variety of World Wide Web 'home pages' were produced from across disciplines and departments and the interested reader who can access the Web is referred to the report written for DEET given below to locate these pages.

Evaluation

Course participants were asked to evaluate the success of the programme, by using the medium in which they had been training, namely using the Web as an interactive medium with fill-out online forms. Responses were collected and collated; an attempt was made to determine if there were any attitudinal differences between the PC users and the Macintosh users; the Macintosh users were marginally more positively inclined towards the effectiveness of the course than the PC users. I include some comments:

Subject: clickable maps
I'm about to put one of these beasties online and would just like to quickly say (prior to the event) that I am very impressed with your HTML lessons. They are easy to use, yet informative, and that they contain real live working examples is simply excellent. I cut-and-pasted the default URL script you mention, and it worked first time. Yeah!
I have also added a form and a table, both within the same document (I wanted the form to line up). I'm a bit hazy about what happens after the form is successfully sent – it reported 'the following e-mail was sent' etc. I am hesitant to cut-and-paste your 'success' example. The e-mail was sent successfully though – I just got it.
Consider praise, money, lollies and flowers sent, in voluminous quantities!
User 1: accessed the resource online only. Did not attend courses.

This won't assist the questionnaire but I have to say that the only criticism of the course was the last session where we joined the other group. Various members of that group took over the instruction session in what appeared to be a macho contest about who knew the most. They slowed down the delivery of information to others so much that I almost walked out. One person even refused to believe what Geoff Rehn was trying to teach him. If I had been put in that group from the beginning, I probably would not have stayed. As you probably can't throw these ego freaks out of a class, they need to be brought under control by the demonstrator so that we ALL

can gain from these sessions. Apart from that gripe, everything else was great.
User 2: one of the Macintosh hands-on intensive attendees.

Comment: the last session was a combined group looking at image capture and incorporation of images into the Web. The above perhaps clearly indicates the previously mentioned differences in user characteristics, the 'other group' being the fairly sophisticated PC users. Further evaluation can be found in the documentation listed below.

The interested reader is referred to the online material which can be accessed through the World Wide Web. Reference is made to the registration forms, the online course, evaluation forms and also evaluation reports.

References
Skills in creating networked information resources for teaching and learning
   http://cleo.murdoch.edu.au/asu/edtech/asdf95/
Final report compiled for DEET, including participant's home pages
   http://cleo.murdoch.edu.au/asu/edtech/asdf95/report.html
A paper discussing the development of the above online course in depth (rich text file format)
   http://cleo.murdoch.edu.au/asu/edtech/pubs/rehn/Ed699_Independent_Study.rtf
The design of the online survey instruments (rich text file format)
   http://cleo.murdoch.edu.au/asu/edtech/pubs/rehn/Ed623_Instrument_Design.rtf

Chapter Fifteen

Text, theory, event: Interactive CD-ROM technology for the humanities

Lisa McRory

The 'Text, Theory, Event' project is investigating how visual and interactive design can best be used to present a variety of primarily print-based archival materials and supporting contextual information. It uses journal extracts (text), critical discussion (theory), and historical material (event) to create an interdisciplinary study of issues of gender and race in relation to Victorian women's periodicals. The final product will take the form of a CD-ROM that will support lecture and seminar programmes in the school of Media, Critical and Creative Arts (MCCA) at Liverpool John Moores University (LJMU). It could also form the basis of seminars, projects, and private study and serve as a general arts and humanities library resource.

Feedback from people who have viewed and used the 'Text, Theory, Event' *Alpha* prototype suggested that the most successful screens were those that integrated primary material from the highly individual LJMU Liddell-Hart archive, or presented related factual information in an interesting way. As a result, it was decided to foreground, and make more extensive use of, the unique primary materials so close at hand in the archive – namely works directly concerning fashion, feminism, the psychology of dress and society at the turn of the century. Period journals from this archive, particularly the Victorian women's periodicals, now form the main primary resource bank for the *Beta* prototype of the CD-ROM. Traditionally, microfilm has been used to make delicate documents and archival material accessible. However, microfilm lacks the ability to reproduce the quality of print and paper. 'Text, Theory, Event' uses image digitisation technology to overcome these limitations.

If the project were only concerned with capturing, cataloguing and presenting facsimiles of the journals on-screen, a simple database holding digital images of the pages would serve the purpose. It is, however, the placing of the texts within a supportive structure of secondary resources that adds dimensionality and context, and justifies the use of the term 'multimedia' when describing the 'Text, Theory, Event' system. The following sections will outline the process of constructing a working prototype for the system, and will then enlarge upon some of the key issues involved.

A working prototype

Developing a working prototype for the Text, Theory, Event CD-ROM included the following steps:

capturing the archival materials, which involved:

- photographing selected pages from the journals;
- processing the negatives onto photo CD, a system which makes computer images from film transparencies (high street film developers do this);

cleaning up' the digital images using Photoshop, an image manipulation package, resulting in high quality images and clean text, easily readable on screen;

designing appropriate interface mechanisms to:

- allow viewing of the journal pages on-screen;2
- enable the user to 'dive down' into chosen contextual information – an example of this is the 'print technology object' – a nineteenth century periodical, rendered on-screen in a tactile, three dimensional form; interrogation of this 'object' reveals video clips, audio tracks, text, and examples of print media which together chart the mechanisation of the print process through the 1800s;

building the system   using the multimedia authoring package *Director*, necessitating both programming and design expertise; *Director* is a dual platform package; that is, it runs on both a Macintosh and an IBM-compatible PC;

building the interactive 'objects'   and embedding them into the overall system design; this involved finding or creating the necessary resources, be they voice-overs, video-clips, still images, text, animation or 3-D modelling;

Practical issues

The production team

Text, Theory, Event is a collaborative project between LJMU's Learning Methods Unit and the Multimedia Courseware Development Group which is based in the School of Media, Critical and Creative Arts. The Learning Methods Unit has already produced a number of extremely successful multimedia products. From past experience, staff at the unit believe that a range of skill-sets are needed in the development and production of multimedia, a predominantly *visual* form. In accordance with their philosophy, the Text, Theory, Event team included a content researcher, designer, programmer and audio-visual producer. The content researcher was involved in decision making throughout the prototype stage; indeed, control of the production process has been shared by all parties, but the senior multimedia designer has held a pivotal role in the creation of the look and feel of the system.

Copyright

Like all electronic publishing projects, Text, Theory, Event has had to deal with the copyright status of resources and materials used. The viability of the project has, to a large extent, been dependent upon the fact that our major resource bank is both owned by the university and consists largely of materials which fall outside the 70-year copyright law.

Funding

Producing a multimedia CD-ROM is expensive, in terms of both time and resources. The project is currently funded internally but, when the latest prototype is completed, decisions regarding further funding will have to be made. To this end, work in progress has been presented to various commercial publishers. They were, however, more familiar with broad-based, encyclopaedic systems on CD-ROM, and generally felt unsure about committing to a tightly focused, academic project of this nature.

Involvement of academic staff

Enthusiasm for the project has been expressed by various academic staff members, particularly those with related research interests. In a large teaching-led university, however, with limited time for personal research projects, whether or not the CD-ROM will enhance the individual/institutional research profile – ie, will be commercially published – has been a key factor in determining involvement.

IT literacy

Evaluation findings from previous initiatives in the humanities computing field at LJMU have highlighted the lack of IT literacy amongst humanities students and staff. These findings have led to the realisation that if humanities computing software is to be used by staff and students, and eventually integrated into programmes of study, a concerted effort to address the issue of IT training would have to be made. Accordingly, at the beginning of the 1995/1996 academic year, first year students in the Arts and Professional Studies division were given an official (two-hour) introduction to the university computer network and the Windows interface. Whilst this was an improvement upon the non-existent computer induction arrangements of previous years, it must be recognised that if students are going to have the confidence to exploit electronic learning resources, *ongoing* support and training, especially for those not traditionally drawn to IT through their subject area, is fundamental.

Where to now?

The range of skill-sets involved in multimedia production necessitates team work and communication between the various specialists working on a project. This team approach has been crucial to developments in the 'Text, Theory, Event' project so far. To take the project out of the prototype phase, funds will be needed to maintain the same degree of expert staff commitment. If development does continue, then trialing the completed prototype with end-users would be the next step. Such trials would necessarily inform the development cycle by producing valuable feedback regarding the design, functionality and content of the system. Production costs in terms of time and money will then need to be weighed against benefits, pedagogic and commercial, to determine the future direction and viability of the project.

Sources of information

Humanities computing yearbook

Computers and the humanities – journal

CTI Centre for Textual Studies – special publications eg, *The digitisation of primary sources*

The MCCA Multimedia Courseware Development Group's WWW home page can be found at: **http://www.livjm.ac.uk/on_demand/mcdgroup.htm**. It includes links to some of the best humanities web resources that we have found.

Chapter Sixteen

IT training by satellite

Adrian Vranch

This case study describes research at the University of Plymouth to explore the potential, to training, for the integration of the technologies of live satellite transmission, computer graphics presentation for interactive audio conferencing and video conferencing. The research was funded internally by the university Staff Development section and the Computing Service and externally by the European Space Agency and has been developed in a number of phases, starting in 1993, and is still on-going in 1996.

In 1993 the University of Plymouth extended over four main campuses in Devon, England (at Plymouth, Exeter, Exmouth and Newton Abbot) separated by a maximum of some 100 kilometres. In 1993 there were over 15,000 students at the university, including those studying on franchise courses in collaboration with local partner colleges. Expansion in student numbers raised this total past 20,000 in 1996. This expansion was partly as a result of the addition of regional Health Studies students, which also added more campuses to the University, increasing the extremes of separation (now Camborne, Cornwall to Taunton, Somerset) from 100km to 200km. The nature of separation of campuses has highlighted the need to develop effective distance communication and learning strategies for the University and its partner colleges, part of which is addressed by the work described in this case study.

There is a strong focus on staff development within the University. All staff, both teaching and non-teaching, are encouraged to participate in a wide range of staff development courses, covering all aspects of training needs. In particular, there is a demand for courses in topics related to information technology (IT) from staff based at all campuses, delivered mainly as hands-on sessions to groups of staff in computer training rooms.

It was in the context of increasing demand for staff development and training courses in IT, combined with the need to address the problems of travel between campuses, that the present research was instigated to explore the use of satellite in delivery of IT training courses for the University. The established University infrastructure, including a well-equipped TV studio with experienced staff and direct links to the TDS4 satellite broadcast uplink on loan from the European Space Agency, provided a key basis for this work.

The IT training by satellite series: Initial objectives of the pilot programmes

In a joint initiative between the Computing Service, the University Step-up satellite facility and the Personnel (Staff Development) Department, a pilot project was set up in 1993 to explore the potential for delivery of an interactive training programme simultaneously to all four main campuses of the University. Staff development training sessions, covering a range of topics related to information technology, were identified for delivery via satellite in the form of live transmissions to all four campuses. The main focus of the project was to explore the potential for the use of the combined technologies of:

- live satellite transmission
- computer presentation techniques
- telephone conferencing.

The interactive sessions in this pilot project provided participants with the opportunity to question presenters at the university TV studio in Plymouth by telephone. Opportunities for participants to complete hands-on exercises on computer were also encouraged during some sessions.

Emphasis and content of pilot programmes

In each programme that was transmitted in this pilot study, specific aspects of applying the combined technology to training were explored, as appropriate to the content of the session topic. Table 1 summarises the ten training sessions that made up the pilot study. In each one-hour session, there was a main presenter (the author of this case study) and a varying number of studio guests, each an expert in a topic covered in that transmission. The emphasis and content of these programmes fell into three broad categories, all related to aspects of information technology, as follows:

- general interest
- software-specific
- function-specific.

In some cases the category influenced the choice of the room used by participants to receive transmissions and the facilities that were made available. In this way, the sessions with a general interest appeal (eg, computer viruses and Display Screen Equipment Regulations) concentrated on presentations and demonstrations to groups followed by audio conferencing discussion.

Interactive training for specific software packages (eg, Excel spreadsheet) was delivered to groups where some participants were provided with computers and supporting documentation to enable them to complete hands-on exercises during the transmission. Interactive feedback via audio conferencing enabled clarification and in-depth exploration of specific areas.

The third category was provided in the form of function-specific or 'awareness' sessions (eg, creating charts, creating presentations and file transfer techniques) that were not restricted to single specific software packages and included demonstrations but no hands-on practical exercises for viewers.

Viewing facilities for participants

There was a varied range of accommodation available in terms of size and suitability for receiving satellite transmissions. At the Plymouth campus a multi-purpose training room was used, with a capacity for up to 40 people and containing eight IBM PCs used for staff training courses. At Newton Abbot a 40-seat student lecture room was used for the first four transmissions and a 24 -seat computer laboratory containing 12 Macintosh LC computers was used for the remaining sessions. At Exmouth a general seminar room with a capacity for up to 20 was used, in which a few Macintosh

Powerbook (ie, laptop) computers were made available for the 18 February Excel transmission. Due to limitations on space caused by major refurbishment work at Exeter it was possible to receive only the last three transmissions, in a 12-seat seminar room with no access to computers.

Equipment

In addition to provision of computers detailed above, each viewing room was fitted with one or two large TV monitors, audio speakers and audio conferencing microphones.

Facilitators

During each transmission a member of staff was present in the capacity of 'facilitator', to supervise the use of the audio conferencing equipment in each viewing room and generally to assist staff who were participating in the programme. The facilitators, who were paid volunteers from library and administrative posts, also helped in the distribution and collection of feedback questionnaire forms that formed an important part of this study. Training, which was given to facilitators in the setting up and operation of the audio/visual equipment in the viewing rooms, was seen as a key element to the success of the project.

Collection of feedback from participants

Feedback from participants was collected in three forms for each session. First, the facilitators noted the total number of staff present and invited comments which were recorded onto a feedback form. This procedure is standard for all satellite transmissions. Second, an attendance list was passed around inviting participants to give their name and department. Finally, each participant was handed a single page questionnaire inviting comments on various aspects of the transmission, including the accommodation, presenter style, session content, workbook content and use of computer graphics for presentation. This questionnaire was deliberately anonymous, so as to encourage uninhibited comment.

Studio techniques and presentation approach

General approach: Although it was intended from the outset to produce a series of transmissions to a high standard, it was not considered necessary to employ a professional presenter. Apart from the savings in production costs it was felt that it was more appropriate that members of the university staff should be involved as main presenter and studio guests in this research study, to encourage a closer rapport with the viewers. Depending on the topic of the transmission, there was a blend of formal introduction using the AutoScript device, studio discussion, unscripted presentation (prompted by the use of computer graphics controlled by the presenter and audio conferencing with the participants. Each transmission was taped for future reference.

Equipment: Again, depending on the session, equipment used in the studio included: overhead camera, three main studio cameras, Macintosh LCII with a Mediator video interface and Opus 386sx PC with video interface. The Macintosh was used extensively to provide live computer graphics, acting as a prompt for the presenter and studio guests, as well as providing transmitted output to the viewers, at the discretion of the studio director. In addition to demonstrating appropriate software (eg, Excel spreadsheet examples), the Macintosh was used to provide general presentation graphics, created using Course Builder multi-media authoring software.

Results from the pilot series

Level of participation

Table 1 shows the total number of participants in the University viewing rooms for each transmission. A total of 212 staff participated in eight transmissions. In addition, the programmes were received by staff and students from outside schools and colleges, who viewed the transmissions but did not contribute to the audio conferences and are not included here.

Table 1. Programme details for pilot series (*postponed due to illness)

Programme title	Date	Studio guests	Viewers
Computer security and the virus threat	21/1/93	1	15
Display screen equipment regulations	28/1/93	2	38
Desk top publishing – Elements of design	4/2/93	2	55
Desk top publishing – Using DTP software	11/2/93	2	29
Excel – An introduction for beginners	18/2/93	0	30
Excel – Functions, charts and data processing	25/2/93*	0	0
Excel – An introduction to writing macros	4/3/93*	0	0
How to create charts and graphs on a computer	11/3/93	1	10
File transfer and integration between applications	18/3/93	1	11
Creating presentations on paper and on screen	25/3/93	1	10

The first transmission was not publicised as well as the others and this may have contributed to the low level of participation. After the steady increase in numbers of participants in the second and third programmes there was drop in attendance for the fourth transmission. Some staff felt that the level of the third transmission was set too high for their practical needs and this probably prompted them to miss the fourth programme (ie, Using DTP software). Ironically, the content of this fourth transmission was probably more appropriate to their needs for DTP training.

The need to postpone the sixth and seventh transmissions due to illness seems to have had a significant effect on attendance later in the series. Tapes of previous programmes in the series were transmitted on these two dates and no figures for attendance were collected. It was difficult to let potential participants know when the live transmissions were due to be restored.

Profile of participating staff

Table 2 shows the profile of staff participating in the University viewing rooms. The general distribution of participants was as intended, with a high proportion of non-teaching, support staff.

Table 2. Profile of staff viewers of the pilot series

Category of staff	Percentage of total viewers of the pilot series
Secretaries	27
Other administrative staff	21
Technicians	10
Lecturers	8
Computing service	24
Visitors	10

The high percentage of Computing Service staff reflects their interest in using innovative methods for staff development and training. Four of the studio guests came from the Computing Service. The visitors were from a local business in Plymouth.

Comments from participants

The main feedback from participants was provided from the questionnaires, with 60 per cent of questionnaires completed and returned. Additional comments were received from informal discussion and meetings of user groups.

Generally, the overall reaction from participants to the series of transmissions was very favourable and encouraging. The speed at which the feedback questionnaires were returned made it possible to incorporate suggestions for improvements from one transmission into the next session the following week.

The level of use of the interactive audio conferencing facilities was disappointingly low for a number of reasons. First there were operational problems due to incorrect setting up of equipment or problems with telephone line links. These problems were partly addressed by extra training for facilitators. The second reason was psychological. A number of participants found that the arrangement of the viewing room and the unfamiliar technique of audio conferencing made them hesitant in asking questions.

The use of the Macintosh computer for general presentation graphics was well-received by the viewers and by the production team. The technique of using this computer as a live prompt for the presenters and studio guests was very successful and easy to implement from a studio production viewpoint. Choice of colour combination and type size were both found to be very important in providing a clear presentation that viewers could read with ease. The use of screen menus with hidden buttons for navigation on the Macintosh was very effective in providing an effective but flexible form of presentation.

The use of the Macintosh and the 386sx PC to demonstrate specific software packages was also very successful, although in the case of spreadsheets and other data tables, the size of characters on the screen was too small for viewers to read at first. This problem was later rectified.

Comments on the style of the main presenter and studio guests were generally favourable, with some exceptions. The overall view was that the presentation style was good, relaxed and professional, although some comments referred to 'nervous' presentation and the need to 'smile a bit more'. There was no feedback suggesting that a professional presenter should have been used.

There were some problems related to the marketing of the series that were identified in some of the feedback forms. Some staff felt that the wording of the posters advertising particular sessions did not match their perceived content of the programmes. The nature of a live satellite transmission means that there will be a wider range of experience in the staff attending than would be expected in a standard training session. In this way, it was common to find novices, beginners and experts all watching the same transmission and all with a different expectation of what they would gain. By using the medium of live satellite transmission it was possible to provide general awareness, introductory detail and advanced tips all in one programme, although individuals were made conscious of their own level of ability.

On a different level, in the 18 February Excel transmission, introductory training materials were provided in the form of a 20-page workbook containing exercises. Some participants had access to a computer for this session and an attempt was made to cover the exercises in the workbook by transmitting the contents of the studio Macintosh screen, enabling the participants to follow in an interactive demonstration.

Some participants succeeded in keeping up with the exercises by following the workbook and live demonstration on the TV monitor and using their computer. Others experienced difficulty in coordinating activity on the computer screen, the TV monitor and the workbook and thought the exercise was a failure. Bearing in mind that the workbook takes two-and-a-half hours to complete in a formal training session, it was not surprising that some difficulty was experienced. On the other hand, some staff found the live transmission to be very useful as an overview of the workbook content and reported that this improved their understanding of the exercises when they attempted to complete the workbook later in their own time. In later programmes a two-page help sheet was provided to summarise the key points from the workbook and this was more easy to use during the live transmission than the full workbook.

Again, this shows the importance of recognising the fact that there will be differences in ability, attitude and aspirations among the participants in a satellite training session.

Outcomes of the pilot study

In setting up any training course it is essential to identify the needs and aspirations of the trainees to ensure that the course content matches their requirements. In the case of satellite training this issue becomes more acute, since the medium can offer the potential to deliver training simultaneously on different levels to staff with a wide range of experience.

The pilot study demonstrated that effective training in information technology topics can be delivered by interactive live satellite as long as careful consideration is given to the content of sessions. Participants' comments must inform marketing of courses to match trainees' needs.

The effectiveness of live satellite training transmissions does not appear to be compromised by using non-professional presenters and these programmes are clearly enhanced by the use of live computer graphics presentations.

The key to realising the potential of the interactive nature of the medium is to pay special attention to ensuring that the audio conferencing facilities are working properly and are provided in a way that encourages participation from viewers. This is a key role of the facilitators and must be emphasised in their training.

Supporting workbooks were shown to be more effective when used with a video tape of the session after the live transmission. A single help sheet comprising a two -page summary of specific highlights from the workbook was easy to follow and effective as supporting material during the live transmission.

Further developments in the IT training by satellite series

Following the pilot series, three further transmissions were made in June and July 1993. This comprised the two Excel sessions that were postponed in the pilot series due to illness, preceded by a repeat of the introductory Excel programmes. Experience gained in the Pilot Series enabled improvements to be made in the approach adopted in these Excel programmes. As well as using summary help sheets in conjunction with the workbook the format of the presentation was changed by the addition of a guest, who followed the exercises live during the programme. This improved the style of delivery in a number of ways and enabled useful dialogue to be included.

Further programmes were developed in the series, summarised in Table 3. The June 1994 transmissions built upon experience and successes of the previous programmes, adding more ambitious techniques for integrating computer presentations, especially in the multimedia and graphics-based sessions.

Table 3. Programme details for later programmes in the series

Programme title	Date
Excel 4 – Further Features,	March 1994
An introduction to databases,	March 1994.
Creating multimedia applications,	March 1994.
Course builder – further features,	June 1994.
Introduction to Microsoft Access database software,	June 1994.
Working with colour graphics and images,	June 1994.
Computer security and the virus threat – Update,	June 1994.
Excel – An introduction for beginners,	June 1994.
An introduction to multimedia,	October 1994.
An introduction to Excel,	October 1994.
Photoshop,	October 1994.
Computer security and the virus threat,	October 1994

The four programmes transmitted in October 1994 formed part of an experiment into video compression techniques, monitoring perceived quality of reception of programmes where the bandwidth was changed during transmission. This has implications for reducing satellite charges without perceived loss of quality. In the same period experiments were included to explore the potential of combining ISDN video conferencing with live satellite transmission. Again this has implications for providing 'studio guests' at a distance via video conferencing.

An unforeseen demand for tape recordings of the programmes shown in the pilot series and the three Excel programmes that followed led to the development of customised packaging to incorporate the video tape, paper workbooks, help sheets and computer disks. These packs were made available for loan and proved popular with staff (and students) who had not seen the original live transmissions. There was also an unexpected interest shown by dyslexic students in using video tapes of programmes to learn the basics of Excel, in preference to paper-based learning materials.

Conclusions and future work

The present work has demonstrated the effectiveness of combining technologies in live satellite transmissions for IT training purposes and has shown the potential of how materials produced in this way can be used even after the live programme has been broadcast.

Current developments are focused on extending the techniques developed in the present work and applying them to distance delivery of a wide range of training and educational courses. This includes live transmissions to a new network of regional centres across the South West of England, and to new campuses in Camborne and Taunton. Further transmissions are planned in 1996 and 1997 to Euro Study centres throughout Europe. The content of these courses will go beyond the content of the original IT training by satellite series and the courses will cover a wide range of topics. However, techniques developed in the IT training series for integration of computer graphics and video conferencing will be incorporated into these new courses. Now that these techniques have been established it is easier for presenters and trainers to take advantage of them without the need to be highly computer-literate themselves. This has implications for adult trainers who are considering distance learning methods.

A further series of interactive live programmes with a focus on multimedia will be transmitted to Euro Study Centres in 1996 and 1997 as part of an EU-funded project. These will incorporate ISDN video conferencing to enhance interaction with viewers and to enable guest presenters to be included at a distance.

Attention is also moving towards developments for learners with disabilities, including learners with dyslexia and deaf learners. Following the unexpected interest in the Excel video tapes by dyslexic students, additional, specialist programmes are being considered for the IT training series. These will focus on careful selection of text and background colours, fonts and font sizes and audio aids that can help learners with dyslexia or other visual disabilities. In order to provide IT training programmes for deaf learners, trials are under way to find effective solutions to incorporate a signer and summary narrative text into the proven TV and computer screen approach.

Chapter Seventeen

Rural telematics for economic development

Aideen McGinley and Kate O'Dubhchair

This case study describes the experience of a unique partnership between a local district council and a university, coming together to introduce information technology and telecommunications to a peripheral rural community with the objective of technology transfer for economic development.

The community of Fermanagh lies in the extreme west of Northern Ireland. With a population of 55,000 Fermanagh accounts for 3.5 per cent of the total population of Northern Ireland. Overall unemployment rates are estimated to be between 35 per cent and 40 per cent of those of working age. The labour force shows very little female participation. Long-term unemployment (those unemployed for one year or more) is regarded as a serious problem with 43.5 per cent classified long-term unemployed. The cream of the region's young people go off to university and many do not return. By contrast the area is one of great scenic beauty and offers a high quality of life and many 'outsiders' choose to resettle there. In short the county exhibits all the symptoms of peripherality.

Fermanagh STAR

People living in Fermanagh have a very positive and pro-active outlook due in no small measure to the dynamic leadership of the recently-retired Chief Executive Officer of the Council who has shown great commitment to strategic planning. This attitude presented as a readiness to avail of possible opportunities when the Special Telecommunication Action for Remote Regions (STAR) programme was launched in the late 1980s. The Council turned to the nearest University campus for support and expertise and a joint application for funding was submitted. Main STAR funding had been given to the major telecommunications provider, BT, to lay a fibre optic infrastructure. The Council and University bid for associated funding to promote the use of the services. The bid was presented with a regional vocational thrust targeting key sectors where it was felt that telecommunications offered added value and advantage. Just over £100,000 was raised and the project started in September 1988.

Awareness-raising

The initial challenge was to publicise the project and arouse a level of local interest and awareness. In effect this was 'cold selling'. Initially people thought Fermanagh STAR was a newspaper. To get ourselves known we launched a series of Awareness Seminars publicised through the local press. In many ways this was the first testimony to the partnership – the Council provided space and publicity and refreshments and the University a fleet of speakers and hands-on equipment for demonstration and trial. To be honest we were amazed by the degree of interest. The reaction to these events as something new and exciting certainly fired our enthusiasm and was a salutary lesson in realising that one so easily becomes blasé about technology and that such an attitude can be a turn-off to the uninitiated. We followed this stage by the formation of focused sectoral interest groups in tourism, craft and design and transport. These groups were as widely constituted as possible and met as discussion forums, brainstorming within their sectoral area. Both approaches were fruitful but revealed that the base-line was very low. We were probably a little taken aback to discover that not only was there very little use of telecommunications in the region, but also minimal use of information technology within the economic sector. The moral of this part of the story was that it was useless trying to sell the advantages of advanced telecommunications to someone unfamiliar with even the rudiments of information technology. So we had to readjust our sights and start from the bottom up.

Similar problems were experienced throughout the Province and to address this situation a second call came out for 'demonstration sites' with a remit to display STAR to the public at large and to create a public ready to uptake on STAR. Again Fermanagh STAR was successful and was given an extra £50,000 which facilitated a much more active information campaign. We now felt justified in spending on general 'awareness' and committed ourselves to delivering a wide area of accessibility to viewing new technology and its potential. We didn't confine our awareness-raising to would-be local users but also tried to publicise abroad the fact that Fermanagh was an IT Zone. When the Council took a tourism bus on tour throughout Europe we included a STAR stand and used the slogan 'In Fermanagh get away from it all but stay very much in touch'. We also promoted the IT industry locally as an environmentally-friendly industry for such a scenic area.

Setting up shop

Meanwhile, in parallel, we began to move into our premises at the new Buttermarket Craft and Design Centre. We saw ourselves as purveyors of 20th Century craft. We ordered equipment, a set of PCs and printers for general training and an ISDN workstation and moved to appoint a Centre Manager. In March 1989 we became the first site in Northern Ireland to have an ISDN line installed connecting the STAR centre and the University at the Magee Campus and allowing voice, pictures and data to be transmitted simultaneously. Being first is never easy and the installation and early days were fraught with difficulty. One memorable episode occurred when the engineer who arrived to set up the connection at the Magee end kept insisting that the two lines for voice and data should go in different rooms!

Once ISDN/2 was up and running we moved to a new phase of activity. We continued general awareness training but were now able to demonstrate the potential of ISDN to our sectoral groups and to an emerging group of interested small businesses. The novel aspect which ISDN allowed us to demonstrate was that of desktop conferencing. In reality this means the two parties are connected by an audio phone link but additionally can share documents. The example we used was to display a map of Belfast to those in Enniskillen and ask them to use the 'light pen' to mark a particular place. Our colleagues in Belfast then responded by drawing on the map the most straightforward route. The striking feature is of course the potential for group or collaborative work. We had a second demonstration of this by a shared spreadsheet of accounts where our visitors were encouraged to ask the remote party 'what if' questions and watch the effect as the figures were manipulated from a distance. There were limitations imposed here by the newness of the technology. Connectivity is directly in relation to compatibility and for quite some time we discovered that people we could connect to were few and far between depending on the match of ISDN cards, a plug-in extra to the standard computer. We developed a close relationship with our supplier and one other STAR site and used these two nodes for demonstration purposes.

Telecommunications and economic development

Returning to our vocational and economic remit, we realised we could not adequately address all three sectors originally identified in depth. Tourism was being met to some extent by the national tourist board, transport presented more complex problems, and so we targeted craft and design for a number of demonstration projects showing how combined telecommunications and information technology could be used to open up economic development opportunities. For example, we worked on two demonstrations of online marketing: one for a knitwear manufacturer developing an online catalogue to be used in the Italian market; and the other at the generic level of Craftworks in Belfast and London exploring the possibilities of telematic interaction of customer and designer.

Real success however, could only come from convincing individual companies to take the plunge. Over a period of time a nucleus of interested companies emerged. These ranged from a young woman keen to introduce some form of back office teleworking in her local village, to a screen printer liaising with a designer in Devon, to an orthodontist and dentist electronically exchanging images. There were many other ideas but finance was the harsh reality. None of the companies we were dealing with had a computer and few could afford the investment of £3,000-£4,000 necessary for the most basic system and certainly not on a 'this might be useful' basis. We had some hopes that this fact of life had been acknowledged at the centre by the European Union when STAR was followed by Telematique, a programme geared to further uptake of the telecommunications services. However, the detail was disappointing in that the programme only supported telecommunications equipment and charges (ie, an ISDN card or modem and service charges) and made no provision for the fundamental base equipment. Only a small number of our companies were in the position, therefore, to avail of the programme. We also found that translating the requirement of the 'Eurospeak' proposal was potentially a major turn-off and so we hand-held our client companies through the process. The successful companies then in turn subcontracted to us the associated consultancy and training which considerably helped our struggling cashflow. We were lucky with the companies we supported and only had one incident in which a client took the equipment and ran. While this was a difficult and expensive lesson which we had eventually to write off to experience, it had its benefits in that it make us think through the contractual arrangements which stood us in good stead for the future.

On a more positive side, working with the young woman interested in teleworking proved very exciting and rewarding. Through great determination and dedication she managed to gather funding and support for both a greenfield site telecottage and for creche facilities, the first ever in Fermanagh. The Centre supported her terms of credibility, which was the key in securing pilot contracts and in equipment selection and installation and training of an all-female workforce. Today her business is thriving with more than 20 employees and contracts ranging from a mail order company to a graduate recruitment company in West California.

At a general level most importantly Fermanagh began to have an external reputation for telecommunications, for a level of awareness and availability of an infrastructure and of a trained workforce. Not unrelated, therefore, was the creation in Enniskillen, the County town of Fermanagh, of a BT backoffice for Central London enquiries with 240 jobs, and the promise of 150 to follow.

NISTAR

Fermanagh STAR was one of 12 STAR centres funded in Northern Ireland. Quite early on these centres formed a collective grouping, NISTAR, supported by the Local Economic Development Unit, to allow us to bid and negotiate with suppliers. Initially there were plans for all kinds of rationalisation and co-operation. There has been some which has resulted in attracting funding to the central grouping. However, there has also been a degree of rivalry and exercising of proprietary rights. Certainly we in Fermanagh, from a position of strength, have insisted on maintaining our independence. One of the joint ventures led us into video-conferencing and hosting a number of national events. The centre now boasts two sets of video-conferencing equipment and through the University's system, has taken part in conferences with up to eight parties as well as standard point-to-point (one party to another) conferencing. The systems have been used throughout the community by groups ranging from school children to senior citizens and across the private sector.

Evaluation and lessons learned

In assessing Fermanagh STAR it is worth noting that nationwide there was quite a diversity in the initial STAR projects. Ours was the only one based on a university-community partnership. A number were connected with Enterprise centres and had a business rather than technical focus and many of these experienced difficulty in the start-up stages.

At the end of the formal funding period Fermanagh STAR was evaluated the lead site among 12 sites in Northern Ireland with a record of having trained or demonstrated to over 2,000 people. The Centre had also established a niche for itself in the local market and had moved to a small degree of profitability, the income being a variety of EU programmes, consultancy and local training contracts. The project was a success. Looking back we attribute the success of the project to a number of things. Primarily at Council level, the project was initiated by men and women of vision who were prepared to invest in the future. The project was based on the unique partnership between the University and the Council. This gave a high level of expertise and extended resources to the project and not infrequently saw us through the gap between funding allocations. However, without a doubt, the most important factor was a positive attitude which took the project out into, and very firmly gave ownership to, the community. This was backed throughout by a sensitivity to our place in the local scheme of things and that stimulating economic development meant stimulating others to provide some of the services the Centre initiated.

Where next?

At the end of 1994 we literally stood back and said 'STAR is over – we've met our objectives and it's been a success, where now?' The answer was a complex one and involved the University in assisting the Council in the derivation of a Regional Economic Development Strategy. It is perhaps a fitting epitaph to STAR that what emerged were two overarching themes – telecommunications and higher education as the catalysts for regional economic development. Taking this forward involved us in redefining relationships and embarking on a challenging new programme of co-operation spanning the next five years. This will encompass the STAR activity of technology transfer for economic development and foster community development and access to higher education through telematics. To do this we have an ambitious building plan which is also a very symbolic project in a time of cross-community reconciliation. The project is known as Fermanagh Higher Bridges – bridges out to global markets and communities, and bridges across cultural and community divides. Physically this entails the refurbishment of the Old Protestant Orange Hall, a listed building, as an Interactive Technology Centre (INTEC) and in a new building on the adjacent site of the Enniskillen Poppy Day bomb blast, the Roman Catholic Reading Rooms.

The focus of Fermanagh Higher Bridges is still firmly rooted in the community and the project is managed by a University Partnership Board with representation from all sides and from the public and private sector. In advance of the completion of the building a modest academic plan has been launched and approximately 100 places on part-time programmes of study will be offered this year.

In response to identified local need these programmes offer professional development, wider access to HE through telematics and a higher degree of local HE provision.

Alongside Higher Bridges the University and FDC are working together on a regional information strategy and an innovative and exciting project on community economic modelling. The latter reflects an exciting spin-off from our collaboration and is work we are undertaking with colleagues from the University of Missouri (UM). UM is a large land grant university with a similar rural development and outreach mission to the University of Ulster. UM had developed a community partnership model with the town of Poplar Bluff in the extreme South of the State and has opened a Telecommunications Community Resource Centre (TCRC). As part of co-operation between the two universities, Fermanagh and Poplar Bluff have twinned and this now offers opportunities for exchange of best practice between the two regions.

Conclusion
In this kind of work it is difficult at any point to draw a line. However, looking back over the last eight years there is a sense of achievement. Fermanagh could now be described as regionally IT literate and ready to participate in the Information Society in terms of Advanced Telecommunications and Technology (AT&T). The Interactive Technology Centre will further enhance the local technological resource, and the continuing partnership provides the vehicle to optimise the facility. Much, however, remains to be done and we look forward to an exciting future with new projects and continued growth through telematics.

Chapter Eighteen

Rural broadnet in Shropshire

Sue Challis

The University of Wolverhampton's Rural Broadnet project is designed to explore the feasibility of using information communications technology (ICT) to overcome barriers to accessing education, training and other opportunities which may arise from rural isolation or tradition.

The project is funded from the Higher Education Funding Council for England's 'Widening Provision' fund for four years, and, at present, we consist of a full-time Project Officer, part-time Researcher (considered an important part of the project) and two half-time Outreach Workers based in the field. Initial research suggests that there is already a voiced demand in rural Shropshire for certain sorts of courses, particularly NVQ Level 2 and 3 in Childcare or Playwork, the preparatory learning which precedes these (plus necessary study skills), business start-up skills, and fairly basic IT skills, including NVQ Telematics.

Our target groups are communities which are geographically isolated, and within them particularly women returners and the young unemployed. Our brief is not to provide training ourselves, but to identify cases where the new technology can be used to facilitate access to training which otherwise would not have been provided. This means that we tend to work in partnerships (for example, with the local Pre-School Learning Alliance in a remote area where scarcity of students and travel problems make it too expensive for them to run the NVQ Level 3 Childcare and Level 2 and 3 Playwork courses which six people have requested). It is hoped that the needs can be met through a mixture of IT-based distance learning (using for example, the National Extension College's NVQ Portfolio Building software), video-conferencing, e-mail and split-site teaching. In addition trainees will attend basic computer familiarisation courses alongside a group of other local residents keen to learn how to use their new 'electronic village hall' which we have helped to equip.

Local background

Shropshire is a large, mainly rural, county with a population spread at about half the average UK density and a low participation rate in non-statutory education. Many communities are distanced from continuing educational and training resources by lack of transport, time and money. Other factors, such as lack of experience and tradition, may also play a part. The decline of traditional farming activity has led to low morale and even a rising suicide rate in certain isolated areas.

Local people do not necessarily see their location as a problem: for example, local firms – nearly half of which employ less than seven people – are positive about Shropshire's central position and the high degree of local customer loyalty. Very few of them identify a lack of IT as a problem. Lack of available finance is identified locally as the biggest stumbling block to economic development and youth out-migration as the most pressing social problem.

Community-led or technology-led ?

No matter how 'virtual' an institution can be made by new technology, the need to establish a local identity remains – particularly in remote areas where even communities seven miles away can seem quite foreign. The Rural Development Commission is convinced that links between people don't follow electronic networks (however much these may enhance communication) – they precede them. At the time of writing the Project has only just begun, but we have already started to come to grips with some of the implications of the phrase 'community-led' inserted rather blithely into our original bid. We have discovered that not only must we uncover and build on existing relationships between individuals and groups in the original communities we approach, but also new networks must be developed through personal contact – despite the more romantic assertions of the 'electronic superhighway' buffs.

Making early contacts in South Shropshire (a particularly isolated rural area with a population density among the lowest in Europe and hills that spell trouble for satellite technology!) we soon realised that there was a wide range of voluntary and paid 'fieldworkers', often covering overlapping geographical areas or with similar aims. South Shropshire is well researched – almost 'researched-out' – by bodies seeking European funding, and so on. Some of the local workers we met expressed concern at what they saw as a burgeoning outreach industry, in which complementarity and established local networks could be neglected.

Our first workshop day, 'Can IT help local work?' drew over 40 local fieldworkers, volunteers and 'community activists', from the Women's Institute, churches, village halls and magazines, from local private and public trainers and community educators, and from an unusually wide range of community and youth work agencies operating locally. Working with University, Training and Enterprise Council (TEC) and District Council staff, we offered hands-on experience and demonstrations of ICT – lots of internet links, multi-media, video-conferencing, databases, distance learning, OHP-computer links, printers and laptops.

Lunch provided a much-welcomed opportunity to talk – not often available, even to people working in the same or nearby patch, with similar aims and target groups. Ideas flowed: from video-conferencing to teaching people how to use information points, to ways of integrating and updating existing databases, and so on.

A clear message came from the afternoon sessions: consultation at local level is vital, within organisations and regions – and the big fear is that imminent decisions about IT infrastructure will be made without it. Participants felt that the extent to which local people have control over ICT is as important as access to hardware and information – adding that the most versatile and cheapest technical option might also be the most financially sustainable and therefore the most open to local control. A forum to promote consultation and collaboration was set up on the day and already a series of trips to rural and urban telematics projects is underway.

ICT is powerful, participants felt, but is still a tool, in this case of restructuring determined by economic, social and institutional changes. Needless to say, not everyone in the University would agree: some, working at the pioneering cutting edge of electronic technology, see it as a prime motivator of changing relationships. This tension has led us to a two-tiered strategy. On the one hand, we are trying to develop an overview of future directions, focusing on matching needs research with long-term, county-wide or regional hi-tech solutions, concentrating on issues such as inter-operability – the interconnection of networks, services and applications and second-guessing market trends. This overview links our project with the University's much grander urban Broadnet in the Black Country, where research and design are prime, and forms a good deal of our work with local organisations.

On the other hand, we are trying to build up a picture of local communications and training need and existing local IT capability and expertise and to explore ways of working with and enhancing these, however short-term (as the technology changes) they may prove to be. The bottom line for a village project is a secure room, electricity supply and telephone line – not always available – to which we can bring a laptop and modem. Although speed and picture quality can sometimes be inferior, we are using a POTS (Plain Ordinary Telephone System) Video Conferencing kit because it is cheaper and doesn't require a costly ISDN line. Although we agree that there is no point teaching people on outdated software, particularly if they are looking for employment or business links, we will use disk-based learning materials as well as CD ROM, until CDs become truly 'universal'.

Planning technical support for a project which will eventually extend all over Shropshire has been difficult. Should we look to 'outsource' locally (perhaps in areas where local education and training providers have already overstretched their techni-cians and appropriate skills may be scarce) or should we make a demand for unprecedented flexibility on the University's centralised technical support systems ? We'll probably do both: meanwhile, the problem exercises a beneficial pressure on us to look for user-friendly, relatively simple technical solutions.

The pilots

Our pilots could be described as action research to develop models of local work. We first looked for an existing local organisation which had already identified education and training needs hampered by features of rural isolation, such as distance, low popula-tion density and low income. We are now working with the Shropshire Pre-School Learning Alliance (SPSLA), who run training courses for parents and playgroup organis-ers. Their courses – from short, informal sessions on play to the NVQs mentioned above – are in great demand, particularly now with European rulings and the need for qualified staff to meet nursery voucher requirements.

They have identified areas where IT might be useful: TDLB and NVQ portfolio building for tutors and students; study skills for pre-diploma students; and, for playgroup committee members, organisational skills such as formal letter writing, accounts, spreadsheets, databases and minute taking. Although there are various local providers of these kinds of training, cost and lack of transport prove a barrier to many potential students – particularly mothers with young children.

We are working with residents of a tiny village, Newcastle on Clun, whose ambitious but locally-rooted vision and hard work have resulted in the construction of a new community centre. The centre will have childcare faciities, a frail-and-elderly centre, theatre, a youth club and a fully-equipped telecentre with ISDN links to urban firms. As well as identifying 10 childcare students for the SPSLA training, they hope to train six local women as data inputters, providing work which will keep families in the village. NVQ Level 2 Telematics courses will be offered this year (1996). Our project is loaning five Pentiums plus Windows 95 and Office software, a Deskjet 1600 colour printer (good enough for local business use), four modems and a video-conferencing link. Because Newcastle on Clun is so poorly served by analogue telephone systems the project is also lending five 'uninterruptible power supplies'. South Shropshire District Council (which funded most of the development) is currently rebuilding several village halls to a standard of security which will enable IT development, providing communities with 'electronic village hall'.

Our second pilot project provides an outreach worker in a new IT resource centre in a small market town, a place where the drive to secure local, regional and European funding and then dispose of it has sometimes seemed to exacerbate divisions within the community. The IT resource centre will be privately managed and partially financed by the income from craft unit lettings.

While the centre is under construction, we saw the chance to try out a video-conferencing kit as an opportunity to expose some of the local divisions and look for ways of promoting the co-operation essential for the local project's success.

We were pleased that people who, at the start of the four-week trial, were reluctant to work together, were intrigued enough to join the trial – and that others, who, theoretically, could have made contact at any time, used it as a way of making links for other purposes. We used a POTS kit to facilitate both a video image exchange and sharing software. Three local students who currently travel over 50 miles a day by bus to Shrewsbury FE College were able to talk over a 45-minute period to their tutors there and work on text and graphics on-screen with their tutors. The downside was the timelag on the video image, which the younger users found particularly distracting, and several occasions when the link failed, signalling 'poor line quality' .

During the trial most links lasted about 15 minutes and were simply explorations of the technology. No one responded to invitations in the local shop and library, but most people we asked personally did have a go, among them a Community Council fieldworker, FE IT and flexible learning tutors, community and adult education workers and Community College careers, physics and IT teachers. A particularly useful link was made between the University's HE advice shop in Wolverhampton and a group of sixth form students who came prepared with questions about university applications. One link involved an autistic student, described by his tutor as having 'extremely limited interpersonal skills', who was reported as being willing and able to communicate through the system with more confidence than usual, verbally, graphically and textually.

The system seems to work best on a 486 with a one-megabyte graphics capability and at least four megabytes of RAM. On a machine with only half a megabyte of graphics the visual image was distractingly poor. BT denied 'poor line quality' had anything to do with them. Perhaps it was the analogue exchange telephone lines, or maybe we'd installed it wrongly? The system worked well when the company demonstrated it! We will continue to investigate, but, either way, it's clear that IT failures, as well as successes, can draw people together.

The virtue of a POTS kit – as opposed to one using a dedicated phone line which must be installed and rented – is its low cost: about £900 an 'end'. It can also be moved around easily, as long as you know how to install software. A big disadvantage is that it's not compatible with ISDN systems, currently more commonly used in rural (and urban) education and training centres – although the manufacturers of this particular system assured us that a ISDN conversion kit will soon be on the market. Meanwhile, we intend to lend the system to a local FE College to facilitate some of the childcare training – particularly the underpinning knowledge and understanding elements – across 40 miles of Shropshire hills.

Where next ?

Our project made links with a variety of organisations. We hope to 'supply' an undergraduate tourism and marketing student to a community school which is developing a strategy for its community IT resource centre, using local suppliers, and needs to consolidate with some market research – but students who will work for next-to-nothing in rural areas are few and far between. However, a post-graduate Informations Systems Engineering student is working with the District Council in the rural hinterland of Telford to identify training needs and potential IT solutions.

Discussions with various local fieldworkers have led to the concept of ROCS – Recycle Old Computers in Shropshire! Our idea is to offer older, but still working, computers to groups whose members might be deterred from taking the initial steps into IT because of the potential to damage or lose expensive equipment, lack of security or insurance and so on. We intend to support a network of voluntary technical help for this project.

Meanwhile, the 'electronic village hall' will be very expensive to equip – but local residents believe they have a business plan which will lead to sustainability in the longer term. We'll follow this development very closely, since it is close to the heart of the Rural Broadnet project.

References
Cooke, P & Price, A (1995) *Telematics and Rural Development* Centre for Advanced Studies, University of Wales, Commissioned by Rural Development Commission

Chapter Nineteen

Using telematics to take the 'distance' out of distance learning

Brian Gilding, Paul Helm and Rob McClements

The Bradford Case Study demonstrates the use of currently available communications technology, satisfying the needs of learners by taking the 'distance' out of 'distance learning'. The project team has effectively responded to market pressures to provide executive learners with multimedia.

The progress made by the Bradford Management Centre in developing the use of multi media in an open, distance learning environment relates closely to the reasons for entering the field in the first place. The Management Centre is a full-range Business School, and the Executive Development Programme has been internationally recognised for over 25 years. An essential part of the success of the Programme has depended on our adjusting quickly to the demands and needs of corporate clients – in the main, the major companies in the UK.

Some eight years ago it became clear that, following the slimming-down of management ranks in the eighties, client companies were seeking a new approach to developing their executives entailing rather shorter periods of residential courses, together with some individual in-house or company-based work. Over the next four years the methods and techniques available for delivering 'student-centred' open learning at a distance were reviewed and focus groups were set up with the major clients. The clear conclusion of the study was that such methods were unsatisfactory, particularly where senior managers were the students, for three reasons.

- The learning material is static, in the sense that it was so expensive to create, and so expensive to update or modify, that updating did not occur and material soon became dated.
- Interaction between the students and the material was programmed, in the sense that student questions had to be predicted and written into a familiar CBT framework.
- The learning experience was a lonely one.

Senior managers and their companies found such a process unacceptable and therefore attempts to integrate residential learning with individual distance learning offered little chance of success. In an attempt to develop an educational capability to include effective distance learning, a research and development project was launched in 1988. The result of that project is an educational process that can meet the three objections and can offer an effective *integrated* approach to executive development which is also appropriate for closely-related activities in executive MBA and other MBA programmes.

Any learning process involves the distribution of facts, interpretations and opinions from tutors to learners, opportunity for student learning through using the material, and interaction between student and tutor to extend and consolidate the learning. The original intention was to create a multi-media package, as it was then understood, to deliver the learning. The subsequent growth of communications technologies such as the WWW and ISDN have been absorbed into the project and are being built into the programme.

A particular strength of Executive Development is the close involvement of tutors, or facilitators, with the executives. That is why residential courses are usually delivered to small groups of managers, frequently by two or more tutors. In order to try and maintain this personal link, it was decided to feature tutors and advisors in the multimedia learning material, with the same people involved in the various interactions between tutors and learners. The tutors involved soon realised that a rather different set of teaching skills was required for this type of work as opposed to traditional teaching and there was a certain amount of tutor resistance and anxiety.

The recent advances in bandwidth now mean that the course designer does not have to worry overmuch about how much data to include in the learning package. They can include whatever they think relevant, whether it is text, audio or video. One of the stages of the learning process in which multimedia may well be superior to lectures or paper-based materials is in the student's initial exposure to the subject. Now that technology has finally caught up with tutor's imaginations, and students are more computer-literate, we can expect to see this superiority made explicit and consolidated.

The updating of the teaching material implies that it is stored centrally in some way, and transmitted through the communication system. The centrally-stored material could be updated at will, and recent, volatile information added whenever it appeared. That is still the longer term aim, but in this early stage we have set up a means of testing out our ideas by storing the material on a CD and making the CD available to learners in the test situation.

So far two such 'course modules' have been created: an elementary Economics module and a Strategic Management Case Study based upon the remarkable success story of Hewlett-Packard's experience in the UK in recent years. Other modules are currently in preparation, and the learning process is being tested using CDs in circumstances which closely model those which will soon be the norm in Executive Development and MBA work.

The most recent experience has been with the Hewlett-Packard Case Study, and a brief description of that test will help to clarify the approach. The production of the case study CD owes a very great deal to the support of Hewlett-Packard, and in particular Nick Earle, Hewlett-Packard's European Marketing Director, Computer Systems Organisation. All the information and analysis we needed was made available, and Nick Earle himself agreed to 'feature' in the CD. The case itself was 'written' by our specialist faculty and the head of that section also appears on the CD. The CD was in production over quite a long time, and more and more media were added as the project proceeded.

To test the effectiveness of the learning process the distance learning was simulated by asking our current MBA students to take part as follows. The CD was made available to the students for unsupervised study. In the event, small groups of students worked through the material in about an hour or two.

As with all case studies, there followed a plenary session – in this case the plenary was arranged in one of the normal teaching rooms with an internal tutor leading the session. The room was linked by video conferencing to Nick Earle's office in Bracknell, and he was able to observe the first part of the case discussion, after which the video conferencing signal of him was projected onto the large screen and he was able to take part in a further discussion session on the case. The video conferencing system used at Bradford was BT's VC8000 system, using the PCC software suite, and relayed over ISDN2. Nick Earle was using PictureTel, on a Hewlett-Packard machine. The lecture room is well equipped for audio visual aids, and Nick Earle was projected onto the screen life size. Video quality was good. The students were quick to broaden the discussion into the future of IT, which made the interaction very meaningful and effective indeed. The session was ostensibly a success in terms of cost effectiveness – in fact it is unlikely that Nick Earle could have been involved other than by using the technology. All participants derived much encouragement from this process, to the point where we are determined to increase our efforts in this area. In fact, of course, it is the opinions of the learners that matter and a great deal of information and opinion from the students was collected, and is summarised below.

The main points from the evaluation were that the students were enthusiastic, but thought the experience was 'different' from the traditional method. Whilst they were reluctant to state a preference for either the CD or the traditional method, it was clear that they regarded reading from the screen as less comfortable, and possibly less efficient than reading from paper. Many showed that they are multimedia literate, but that this knowledge has come from games or infotainment software: their knowledge of the capabilities of the technology clashed with what they perceive as important to their course of study, ie they wanted more features, but not too many to distract them. This line of thinking is shown in the enthusiasm for the method of assessment, a quiz. There was evidence of the quiz appealing to the competitive elements, and of learners 'playing the system' – thinking more about the scoring algorithm than the subject matter. In summary, there were problems caused by learning styles and methods suited to traditional delivery being applied to new forms of technology based delivery. The interesting thing is that most of the students were aware of this discrepancy, but unsure of how to cope with it. The discrepancy disappeared during the video conference because the quality of the input (and perhaps the fact that they were in a group once more) made the technology transparent.

The main lessons which have emerged are that the 'personalising' of the material is important. Updating has not been an issue so far. Updating will become an issue and networking of some kind will be essential. Unprogrammed interaction is vital.

The project is now being taken further in two respects. Much has been learned about creating or writing multimedia course material and there appears to be no reason why we should not now go on to write more modules, basing them on faculty expertise in various areas, built up by some 30 years of delivering Executive and MBA programmes. The Bradford Executive MBA is now being delivered in this country to a number of major clients, and the application to those programmes is obvious. In addition, the Executive MBA is delivered in a number of different parts of the world, and the prospect of communicating the multimedia learning to those countries is exciting.

The technology surrounding the learning modules, (that is the methods of accessing the system and the ease with which the user can navigate about the material,) is advancing all the time. Our progress in this respect owes much to the support given by British Telecom, and in fact the Economics module was created with their generous allocation of funds and time. It is our view that we are at the point where this whole development must now be accelerated and to that end we have founded our own European Telematics Group to focus our efforts.

The Case review has confirmed that current technology can provide a learning experience which builds on the best features of traditional teaching – delivered via new media – because the content has been effectively created. The success of the project is based on the importance attached to the content. The interaction between peers and tutors is facilitated by new technology – not replaced.

Section Three

Checklists

You will have found by this stage of the book that the development and delivery of education and training through communication technologies can evidently be rewarding. It can also be demanding, frustrating and time consuming!

When the idea of this book was conceived the main aim was that people with little or no knowledge of communication technologies could pick up the book, develop a feel for how telematics applications could be used in the education of adults and decide for themselves whether this was an area worth pursuing.

Some of the case study authors have indicated that those starting out now are in a worse position as there is less funding available for communications and telematics projects than when they were starting out. This could change; and as the chapter on *The policies and programmes of the European Union* shows, telematics is currently a priority within several EU funding programmes. Furthermore, if a proposal has been thoroughly developed and there is sufficient evidence of need, it is usually possible to find a combination of external funding and internal resources if enthusiasm, commitment and a modicum of innovation are present. One big advantage for people entering the field now is the benefit and hindsight of experience available from those leading the way.

The three checklists that follow provide examples of good practice, pitfalls, and opportunities and benefits. These lists are far from exhaustive, but do provide an overview of practical lessons that can be learnt from the experiences of the contributors.

Good practice

A checklist of good ideas developed from practical experience. Everything included in the checklist has been tried and tested and has achieved some measure of success for those involved in the teaching and learning process.

Staff-related issues

Staff development programmes should be developed and promoted; with courses in familiarisation and then training in usage. Training should be offered in a range of techniques, including e-mail, accessing the Web, effective teleconferencing and using new communication technologies as a teaching resource. Staff ideally need time allocated to acquire new methods of curriculum delivery and time to apply new knowledge.

Having at least one person dedicated to projects and the ongoing development of the use of new technologies is hugely beneficial. This person may co-ordinate those involved, ensure that the project/development moves forward, and devote time to dealing with practical and technical hurdles which will inevitably arise. Where it is not possible to resource a full-time person, find an enthusiast to champion the project developments.

Appoint a project manager who will be involved with the selection, creation and use of materials using communication technologies. Effective project management will curb over-enthusiasm, preventing technological innovations in education from becoming over-ambitious and unwieldy.

Students need access to a 'hot-line', which must be available at regular times. The same member/s of staff may additionally take on the role of trouble-shooter and co-ordinate students' use of the technology. Computer conferences, for example, may be structured, involving introducers, summarisers and secretaries aiming to ensure that everyone participates in the conference. The 'value added' from new technologies will depend very much on the willingness and interest of individual tutors to develop appropriate pedagogies.

Staff without 'technological' backgrounds and expertise have been involved in the development of materials and programmes using telematics applications. Some projects set out to use a mix of IT literates and IT novices to work together on development. A direct consequence of using non-IT specialists is the need to provide training and support for staff.

A firm chairperson is necessary to keep an audio or video conference moving at a reasonable pace and to ensure the participation of everyone involved. Circulating agendas and discussion papers to participants beforehand and agreeing ground-rules at the outset can facilitate effective conferencing.

Where video conferencing is being used by a presenter to give a paper to a group it is beneficial to have a person on location with the group to introduce the presenter and to moderate the subsequent question-and-answer session and discussion.

Scripts circulated in advance and questions submitted beforehand will also contribute to the flow of the conference.

Technical issues: hardware and technical support

The hardware already available (within an institution or community) may not be the most appropriate. A range of issues pertinent to the project may needs consideration, such as 'user-friendliness', equipment, the portability of equipment, running costs, and whether the same hardware may be installed into different locations.

Support from the Information Technology staff and technicians when setting up a new telematics venture is beneficial. This may influence decisions about where to locate any physical centre and with which department or centre to run new programmes or projects. Staff directly involved with programmes using communications technologies may benefit from having access to the basic hardware at home, as well as in their workplace.

Accepting limitations

It is useful to develop an understanding of the practicalities, possibilities and limitations of the technologies, whilst at the same time looking at educational opportunities and objectives which may be enhanced through the application of telematics and other information technologies.

There is a need to be flexible and adaptable when developing programmes using new technologies, as with any innovative programme. Ideas may be considerably modified from the original specification due to technological or resourcing constraints.

Introducing learners to communications technologies

Adult learners inexperienced in accessing telematics applications need a support system that will help them to feel self-confident and self-reliant when using new technology to achieve educational goals.

Tutors and trainers exploiting new communications technologies should provide some form of induction programme for learners. This might involve a hands-on session lasting a couple of hours or providing a brief guidance manual. In-house guidance manuals have been produced and distributed, supporting learners in the installation of equipment and explaining how to use the new technologies. It is beneficial for students to quickly become self-reliant in the use of the technology, and thus active participants in the programme.

A student-centred approach need not be forgotten with the use of communication technologies. There should be structures in place supporting and encouraging students to get the most from new training delivery and research methods. These can range from one-to-one tutor contact, telephone 'hot lines', supporting documentation, creating 'user-friendly' environments and co-ordinating the students' input.

Experience has shown that, where it is possible, learners gain when they meet face to face at the start of programmes where subsequent communication will be through telematics applications. This is particularly true for courses where discussions may be confrontational, or involve those from different ethnic or religious communities.

Partnerships

A number of the case studies have found success through collaboration in developing programmes using communication technologies: eg, between university departments, university and district councils, university and community groups, universities and publishers.

Developing a close relationship with hardware suppliers may provide the opportunity to link up with them for demonstration purposes. Projects involving British Telecom partcipation have found free call charges during all or preliminary stages of the beneficial. Apart from anything else it allows staff to be throughly trained in the equipment, with live experimentation.

Projects and developments which involve the community will succeed when the community has some ownership. This involves consultation with the community, awareness-raising sessions and involving many different groups, community, public and private sector representatives and fieldworkers and volunteers already working in the locality. People with authoring skills and experience can transform and adapt existing materials for the new technologies.

General issues influencing successful outcomes of introducing communications technologies

Support from senior management may be realised through internal resourcing, support for external funding applications or publicly speaking out in favour of the new developments. It can also help if there is a senior manager who understands that innovative projects do not generally become overnight successes, but take time to germinate, develop, pilot and then, hopefully, find a market niche.

Consider venues carefully. Whether for a studio on campus or an outreach centre, issues for consideration include security risks, running costs, accessible technical support, the availability of administrative support (eg to take bookings and hand out materials) and access to potential users.

The benefits of advanced communications technologies cannot easily be sold to those who do not have a grasp of basic information technology. There may be a requirement to start at a basic level in order to gain interest, commitment and consequently the benefit of telematics applications. As with all innovative programmes monitoring procedures, evaluation and time for reflection should be built into the programme.

Pitfalls

A checklist based on the experience of pitfalls that were either encountered or narrowly avoided. To be aware of potential problems saves time and money spent on new developments. It is also possible to create structures and scenarios to avert some of the negative issues identified.

Attitudes

Age has been identified as a factor influencing the individual's decision on whether or not to learn about and use new technologies, for both staff and learners. Generalisations should not be made: there are older staff and learners who enthusiastically embrace and exploit new technologies. And it must not be assumed that younger adult learners know about the new technologies before they begin.

There is some evidence that a lack of IT literacy amongst humanities staff and students, unless addressed, may lead to resistance to the introduction of technology-based teaching methods and resource materials. As well as providing basic level training it may be necessary to address the need for shifts in perceptions.

Anxiety and resistance has been experienced by staff, with the realisation that the use of communication technologies involves a rather different set of teaching skills and the creation of alternative teaching materials. For example, learners have exprssed the view that it is more difficult, or less comfortable, to read off screen than reading from paper.

Equipment

Purchasing and installing equipment always seems to take longer than anticipated: allow for a realistic lead-time. Easy access to the hardware becomes a key issue for learners using communications technologies. At the outset institutions can find themselves in the position of having insufficient resources to meet demand. This can cause frustration, and in turn alienate those who were initially supportive.

Resourcing new developments

The costs of using communication technologies must not be underestimated. These costs relate not only to the initial installation, for which pump-priming funds may have been obtained, but also to ongoing costs such as line rental, maintenance, and additional technician support.

Tutors, who offer learners support through e-mail and computer conferencing technologies, have found the process more time-consuming than communicating with students either face to face or over the telephone. In instances where there are technological problems or where students have problems getting access to computers there is a danger that technology might get in the way of the educational objectives and process.

Teaching materials

New communications technologies can provide the opportunity to do something different. If they are used to replicate what has previously been done using traditional teaching methods of delivery they will be perceived by students and tutors as second best.

Expanding the range of materials and courses available to meet demand may be a problem of success. Organisations may need to employ authors to develop or adapt course materials, and to review existing materials available elsewhere which may be suitable for their market.

It is very easy to make use of all the 'jargon' relating to new technologies; this includes computing terminology and the 'occupational jargon' terms used by those accessing the Web, the Internet and multimedia applications. It can be off-putting, but may also be empowering once understood.

Opportunities and benefits

The final list is a collection of ideas about 'selling the concept of communication technology'. It shows opportunities and benefits that can be gained by organisations, adult learners and tutors using telematics applications for education and training.

For the organisation

Increased enrolment of students due to flexibility offered by new communications technologies.

As well as providing new opportunities for students, telematics may also enhance normal telephone contact for managers and administrators and an alternative way to hold meetings involving staff from different sites.

Offering a more flexible mode of learning can guarantee course viability and thus allow for a wider range of courses and programmes offered.

Multi-campus universities and colleges can reduce the time spent travelling by staff from one site to another, by running courses on two or more sites exploiting communication technologies. Ideally, the tutor will vary the location at which s/he is present, thus ensuring that all students feel that they have personal access to the tutor. This also allows less popular courses to be offered to students based in different parts of the region; which again may allow specialist courses to become viable.

The use of communication technologies provides an opportunity to draw on international expertise, attracting speakers who previously would not have been able to contribute because of travel and time constraints.

Staff development within institutions and groups can creatively and effectively exploit communication technologies; particularly multi-site campuses, Further and Higher Education partnerships or partnerships involving community groups with access to communication technologies.

Training providers may pursue the potential for adapting existing courses (particularly those for which they are renowned) such that they can be delivered and supported through communication technologies. An implication of this is that traditionally-offered courses must keep abreast of developments and market the benefits of attending the course on site (particularly if a reason for success has been that the course is the only one of its type available locally).

For the learner – increased communication

Traditionally, part-time students and adult learners have more limited access to one another than full-time (traditional) students. Telematics applications offer alternative methods of communication and can reduce the feelings of isolation often experienced by this growing student group.

Teleconferencing, computer conferencing, satellite and e-mail provide an opportunity to communicate with people from further afield; from different regions and other countries. This may involve people with different cultures, different backgrounds, and different perspectives being able to discuss and debate issues; providing a wider perspective and an opportunity to consider different viewpoints. Additionally, telematics contributes to the globalisation process, enabling 'star' speakers or individuals to contribute to conferences, seminars and work groups without having to travel (saving on time and financial resources).

One of the constraints of early distance learning programmes is the lack of personal tutor support and opportunity for students to communicate with others involved with the course. E-mail and computer conferencing allows individual tutor support, one-to-one communication between students and group debate.

Opening debates to people from a wide range of backgrounds and experiences through the use of communications technologies will result in contributions from a greater diversity of opinion. There is the potential to benefit from mutual understanding between ethnic groups and to benefit from 'globalisation' opportunities.

Remote specialist expertise is accessible through teleconferencing. This may involve specialist trainer input, or a step-by-step demonstration of advanced practice (eg, telemedicine).

For the learner – increased flexibility

Access to communication technologies can encourage choice and structure through modularisation of the curriculum, self-pacing and interactive feedback.

Using new technologies, such as the World Wide Web and e-mail, adult learners can access education and training at times convenient to them. Learners can work at their own pace. The difficulties of attending regular classes and the need to learn at one's own pace are barriers to learning cited by adult learners, mature students and other part-time trainees. The effective use of communication technologies can resolve a number of these constraints; a case in point of technology providing a solution to educational need. The case studies show examples of the following groups who have benefited from new technologies: rural communities, those with domestic responsibilities and young families, the disabled, small businesses and those who would face high travel costs if attending more traditional courses.

The use of some technologies allows part-time students to enrol throughout the year, thus providing flexible access to education.

Adult learners welcome the autonomy offered by the new technologies; the opportunity to be in charge of their own learning style and to work at their own pace. Some have said that they are able to do more work as a result of not being tied by the constraints of time or having to interrupt work flow or personal life to study.

For the learner – additional skills

One of the key spin-offs from using technologies in the learning process is that students have access to equipment which may previously have been unfamiliar to them; they will gain confidence and experience in using these technologies themselves.

Computer conferencing allows sharing of knowledge and understanding between a group of people who are based in different physical locations. It provides an opportunity for reflection, an informal structure in which to discuss and debate, and allows for the addition of an international dimension.

The Internet offers an additional research tool, with access to wide-ranging sources including libraries, on-line magazines and newspapers, abstracts and specialist data bases. All indications point to continued expansion.

For the tutor

Communication technologies allow for increased communication with students on distance learning courses and/or geographically distant from the institution, both on a one-to-one basis or through group conferencing.

Tutors can monitor students more effectively as they progress through course materials, commenting on drafts of assignments, discussing self-study exercises and encouraging them to communicate with their peers.

Learning materials need not be as static as traditionally-produced materials; it is easier and less time-consuming to update text on screen than printed materials.

Current technology can build on the best features of traditional teaching, delivered via new media, provided teaching methods and materials are created to be used within the new context.

Section Four

Chapter Twenty

Telematics and adult learning

Stephen McNair

Following a national conference in 1995 NIACE decided to review its policy on telematics and adult learning. In Spring of 1996 it published a briefing paper in *Adults Learning,* followed by an invitation seminar to discuss the issues, with 25 people from a very broad range of backgrounds, including FE, HE, government, publishing, broadcasting, libraries and technologists. This paper outlines the strategy which has been agreed following that event, and the issues which emerged from it.

NIACE is the national organisation for adult learning. It exists to promote the interests of adult learners and those who work with them in all sectors and kinds of learning. It has a special concern for those who have benefited least from education in the past, or who are excluded from full participation in society by lack of education.

NIACE carries out research and development work, runs conferences, produces publications and lobbies on behalf of adult learners. Its membership includes most of the organisations working with adult learners in England and Wales, but its distinctive role lies in its overview of adult learners and learning, across all sectors, institutions and modes of learning, both formal and informal, and whatever technologies they may be using.

NIACE and telematics

Developments in telematics raise complex issues for all those involved in education and training. However, adult learning is distinct because opportunities are provided by a much more complex mix of public, private and voluntary agencies, including broadcasters and publishers as well as, increasingly, the entertainment and computer software industries. Whether or not adults have access to learning via telematic routes may depend significantly on decisions made in the markets for entertainment and telecommunications. The principal impact will be in the home rather than the educational institution, and who has access to what may depend as much on decisions about wiring homes as on the organisation and management of schools and colleges.

NIACE cannot afford to ignore the impact of telematics on adult learning, since it is one of the major forces which will reconfigure our understanding of adult learning, how and where it is provided and to whom. It also has the potential to change relationships between individuals and the wider community, in developing areas like 'electronic democracy', and to reshape the roles of education and training providers. It is also a field in which rapid change is endemic, where the policy and technical agenda changes from month to month. Most of those potentially affected are unaware of what issues are important, or even of their existence.

NIACE's particular and unique standing in the debate about telematics is as a voice for the interests of adult learners and those who work with them. This is a function not covered by any other agency, since all others are concerned either with specific market sectors, technologies or sectors of provision. However, it will be essential to keep in close touch with a number of key agencies, including the HE and FE Funding Councils and their associated activities (Higginson, HE Joint Information Services Committee), National Council for Educational Technology, local authorities, broadcasters, Open University, FE Development Agency, and the Library and Publishers' Associations.

Action to date

NIACE's first specific activity in this field was a national conference in 1995, which produced a set of working papers (*Telematics*), and there will probably be further conferences in the future. An invitation consultative seminar was convened in June 1996 to discuss issues and strategy for NIACE .

Since 1996 NIACE has published two books on the subject, *Learners on the superhighway* (a description of current developments in technology based learning for adults in the USA) by Keith Yeomans, and the present book. The Institute is also involved in a range of international activity on this subject, including consultancy work for OECD, which has been reviewing the role of government and institutions in the development of technology-based learning for adults.

NIACE's aims in telematics

The purpose of NIACE's telematics strategy is to ensure that the Institute, and its members, are well-informed about the implications for adult learners of developments in telematics, able to influence those developments, and able to make representations to appropriate agencies. In doing this, NIACE will seek to identify the issues and bring together relevant expertise, informing relevant players as technologies and systems develop. NIACE will evaluate developments and think about futures and options. Throughout all this, NIACE will lobby where appropriate on behalf of adult learners.

In adopting this strategy NIACE seeks to complement the work of the many other (and larger) players in the field, rather than to compete with them. As always, we seek to facilitate and collaborate, and to make sure that adult learners and learning do not get forgotten in the rush to solve the problems of more vocal interests.

Issues

The following issues were identified as worthy of further attention at the consultative seminar which the Institute convened in June 1996.

Policy issues

- networking the various interests – it is important to keep people in touch, to share experience and ideas across organisational divides
- monitoring developments and spotting opportunities – to inform the various fields and formulate policy advice
- coordination and collaboration – to explore ways of encouraging this across boundaries (sectoral, public/private, educators and non-educators, etc.)
- links with the entertainment world – to explore ways of using the power and resources of the entertainment industries creatively

- intellectual property – to contribute to the debate on how to ensure access to knowledge and information without making it uneconomic to produce it
- focus on the consumers rather than producers – to drive institutional change by empowering individual learners
- understanding the potential of telematics and learning in the workplace

Access

- technology as a means of overcoming exclusion – for those whose physical or psychological access problems can be better tackled through technology.
- equalisation of access to technology – to ensure that those who will not get access through private initiative and funding are not excluded
- 'technofear' – understanding peoples' attitudes to the technology, and ways of overcoming psychological barriers

Educational processes

- understanding kinds of literacy – how do people understand and 'read' electronic communication. What about non-text literacies?
- implications of interactivity – how does this transform learning processes, and roles of learners and teachers?

Organisational change

- brokering adult learning – developing strategies for creating learning partnerships, creating virtual learning groups in specialised fields or remote areas
- learning networks – developing the 'National Grid' for adult learning
- guidance – exploring how the technologies can provide better access to information and guidance, and how guidance can adapt to meet the needs of learners who are offered access via the technologies
- accreditation – explore the issues raised by fragmentation of learning, delivery of small blocks and the credibility of accreditation for learning undertaken by technology
- adult use of schools and libraries – explore how schools and libraries can be used as sites for access
- embedding/scaling up projects – identifying previous work which could be developed/embedded

Citizenship and community

- communal and individual learning – exploring models of learning with technology which value the communal as well as the individual
- citizenship – exploring how learning and technology can contribute to a more effective democracy

International issues

- exploring the implications of the globalisation of learning providers for adults – will it lead to diversity and opportunity or to homogenisation and the growth of vast global educational corporations delivering homogenised products?

Resources

- costs/resources and money (how can adult access be funded, especially for the least educated?) – including the use of tax system, universal service models, etc.
- staff development and attitudes – how can teaching and materials development staff be introduced to new technologies and kept up-to-date
- cost-effectiveness – will the technologies make access for larger numbers possible more economically? How and in what circumstances and with what implications for institutional structures?

Content

- quality – address the concern that much technology-based learning embodies poor quality content and pedagogy
- materials production – developing models for more effective use of the technologies, including the involvement of students and part-time staff in this

A strategy for action

The following strategy has now been developed and agreed for NIACE's work in this field:

1. NIACE will continue to be actively concerned with the implications of telematics for adult learners, and will seek to maintain an overview of the full range of policy issues, and a wide network of contacts in interested fields.

2. Within this broad overview, the specific focus will be on issues of access, including both how individuals excluded from education and training can get access to it through the technologies, and how they can get access to the technologies themselves.

3. To achieve these two objectives, NIACE will maintain an ongoing broadly-based telematics policy group, to:

- act as a point of reference for advice on Institute activity;
- advise on NIACE responses to national policy consultations from Government, regulators and political parties;
- assist in planning events;
- provide a forum for members to exchange information and ideas;
- keep the Institute's specific priorities in telematics under review.

4. The group will meet occasionally face to face, to maintain continuity, but in view of pressures on resources and individuals' time, as much business as possible will be done electronically.

5. Membership will be drawn broadly from all agencies with an interest in adult learning (in all its forms).

6. The Institute will, in collaboration with other interested parties, seek to carry out work in four specific areas. In each of these the Institute might bring together interested and/or experienced partners, possibly through seminars or conferences, and might seek to collaborate in research of project work if appropriate:

- **social exclusion** – to explore ways of increasing access through mechanisms like electronic village halls, local learning centres, libraries, workplaces;

- **brokering** - to explore ways of using telematics to enable individuals to identify sources of expertise and develop 'learning exchanges', peer tutoring, virtual study circles;

- **conferencing systems** – to explore ways of using conferencing approaches, both to provide access to learners at a distance, but to create peer teaching and support structures among adult learners;

- **guidance** – to explore ways of using telematics to provide individuals with guidance (not merely information) about adult learning.

7. Where appropriate, the Institute might seek resources to carry out research or development work in any of these areas, in partnership with appropriate agencies

Afterthought

In February 1996 the OECD convened a conference in Philadelphia to discuss the application of new technologies to adult learning. The seminar noted its conclusions, of which the following are particularly relevant to NIACE's evolving strategy in this field:

- in applying new technologies to adult learning the most difficult and expensive issues are human, not technical,
- the technologies are unlikely to reduce social or educational inequality without intervention in the market
- the cultural diversity of OECD states will have important implications for their use of technologies,
- the most appropriate technology is not always the 'leading edge' one,
- education and training systems will need to shift focus from teaching to learning,
- communications technologies will bring fundamental changes in the nature of institutions (including educational institutions)
- communications technologies will bring fundamental changes in the roles of staff.

Chapter Twenty-One

Telematics for education: the policies and programmes of the European Union

John Field

The new information and communications technologies command enormous attention within the European Union. As a result, so many of the EU's activities include some aspect or another of telematics applications in lifelong learning that it is sometimes hard to find one's way through the thicket of initials and agencies. The purpose of this chapter is briefly to sketch the background of the EU's policies in this fast-moving area, outline the EU's priorities, and describe the more important programmes and projects currently funded by the EU. Finally, there is a brief guide to further sources of information.

Current EU policy

Although there were earlier initiatives, current EU policy has developed rapidly since the mid-1980s. In 1984, the Commission launched ESPRIT, the European Strategic Programme for Research in Information Technology, which it had originally proposed to the member states in 1980. In 1985, it launched RACE (Research and Development in Advanced Communications Technologies for Europe). While such initiatives were originally somewhat scattered, they received a significant legislative boost when the 1987 Single European Act added to the Union's Treaty the aim of encouraging 'research and technological development activities', in order 'to strengthen the scientific and technological base of European industry and to encourage it to become more competitive at an international level'. In response, the Commission brought forward a series of four- and five-year framework programmes for research and technology development, each of which has included proposals for the new technologies. Thus by the late 1980s, the EU had acquired both legal powers and a number of specific programmes in this sector (Sharp 1993).

The Union's interest in educational applications developed rather more slowly. Support for distance learning technologies was included within the Third Framework Programme for Research and Technological Development (1990–1994), in the shape of the DELTA research and development programme. At the same time, the Commission was also systematically evaluating the success of such student mobility programmes as ERASMUS and FORCE, which were also developed as part of the move towards the single market from the mid-1980s. One of the conclusions from this evaluation was that the mobility schemes had only affected a relatively small number of people; the Commission therefore proposed to support distance and open learning materials as a cost-effective way of strengthening the European dimension in education (European Commission 1991). When SOCRATES and LEONARDO, the new EU action programmes for education and training, were introduced in 1994, both explicitly placed a high priority on supporting the development of distance open learning through the new communications technologies.

Until the early 1990s, the EU's policies towards the use of telematics in education and training were broadly supportive, but rather poorly coordinated. By the mid-1990s, the Commission was increasingly attempting to develop a consistent policy that would be implemented across all its separate agencies. Partly this was due to changes of senior personnel, and particularly the appointment of Edith Cresson as commissioner for both education and training policy and research policy; partly to recognition among policy makers and their advisers of the far-reaching potential of the new technologies; and partly to a growing fear in both the member states and the Commission that the European economy would be unable to compete with the other advanced industrial nations in adapting to these new challenges.

These anxieties surfaced in 1994 in an important discussion document, *Europe and the global information society* (European Commission 1994), which stimulated a series of measures designed to promote the concept of Europe as an 'information society'. Ideas of an 'information society' or 'knowledge society' were originally devised by journalists and academics to signal the replacement of one type of economy – that dominated by manufacturing industry – by another, in which the leading edge was 'grey capital' (ie, brainpower). In *Europe and the global information society*, the Commission noted that the new technologies are bringing the worlds of production, entertainment and learning more closely together. Subsequently the Commission's White Paper on education and training particularly emphasised the role of multimedia educational software in building a learning society, but also stressed the contribution of the new technologies generally in helping develop approaches that were customised in terms of pace and place, that met the needs of industry as well as learners, and that generated portable skills and qualifications (European Commission 1995).

Primarily, EU policy is to promote telematics-based approaches as a means of fostering Europe's competitivity and growth. Since this is the basis on which the member states came together in the first place, it is not surprising that economic aims continue to dominate the EU's policy agenda. Two of Commissioner Cresson's advisers, noting that the EU moved rapidly to develop a coherent policy after Bill Clinton adopted measures designed to place the American telecommunications and software industries firmly ahead of the global competition, argue that

> In Europe, the search for higher productivity is too often translated into reductions in production costs – bearing particularly on labour costs – rather than into innovation and the conquest of new markets. The sustained pace of the introduction of new technologies into the economy, and the consequent transformation of the productive system, create among other things new skills needs. That requires a capacity for adaptability on the part of workers for which they are insufficiently prepared, and partly explains the persistence of high levels of structural unemployment. . . . Thus one arrives naturally at the conclusion that education and training constitute the key stone of the information society (Riché-Magnier and Metthey 1995, 420).

The most frequently mentioned competitors in this context are the United States and the 'tiger economies' of the Pacific Rim. More broadly, the new technologies are seen by the Commission as extremely important features of globalisation. The White Paper on education and training noted that 'eleporting' – that is, the use of telematics to have work done on-line at a distance from the head office – is leading to job exports to low-wage countries, presenting a major threat to the European social model.

In addition to the overarching goal of enhancing competitivity and growth, though, the EU has a number of secondary aims in developing the use of telematics for educational purposes. One of these is the maintenance of the European social model. Europe, it is argued, cannot follow either the individualistic model of the United States, nor the regimented model of the Asian 'tigers'. The challenge is therefore to adopt the new technologies in such as way as to 'improve the quality of life of Europe's citizens, the efficiency of our economic and social organisation and to reinforce cohesion' (European Commission 1994, 6). At the same time, though, the Union has repeatedly argued that higher levels of growth and improved competitivity are essential to create the wealth upon which its capacity to foster social and regional cohesion will depend.

In addition, there is a strong desire to protect European culture from external – particularly American – influence. Thus the Commission's White paper on education and training expresses the fear of a

> risk that the quality of multimedia products, particularly in educational software, could lead to knowledge of the 'lowest common denominator' in which people lose their historical, geographical and cultural bearings (European Commission 1995, 23).

To some extent, though, this objective of respecting Europe's diversity is in conflict with the aim of increasing competitivity in the global market place. This is because, unlike major software and multimedia producers in the United States and Japan, 'European inventors and industrialists are seriously hampered by the high degree of fragmentation of the market caused by the cultural and linguistic diversity of Europe' (European Commission 1995, 37).

Finally, the EU supports educational applications of telematics as a dimension to other programmes. Examples might include environmental protection, health promotion, or the various initiatives supported under the Structural Funds such as NOW (New Opportunities for Women) and ADAPT (aiming at supporting vocational training in industries where fundamental change and job losses are expected).

In general, the broad priorities of EU programmes are derived from the wider policy goals outlined above:

- developing Europe's competitiveness in the global market place, creating higher growth rates and reducing unemployment in the member states;
- combating social exclusion and enhancing social and regional cohesion within the Union;
- and, though to a markedly lesser extent, fostering the European cultural inheritance.

Priority areas in the EU programmes

In a number of its programmes, the EU is running pilot projects aimed at helping Europe apply the new technologies to teaching and learning. Each programme has a slightly different focus, appropriate to the broad framework within which it operates.

Nevertheless, the EU has become much more concerned to ensure that its different programmes are as coherent and congruent with one another as possible.

Telematics forms a substantial part of the EU's Fourth Framework Programme for Research and Technology Development (RTD4). Here, the overarching priority is to support research which will help Europe's economies withstand international competition and create jobs. Scheduled for the period 1994–1998, RTD4 started in 1995; such delays are usual in EU programmes. For the first time in an EU research and development programme, RTD4 aims to investigate the social challenges of the new technologies.

Educational telematics features strongly in three of the eighteen areas funded through RTD4. The newest of these is the Targeted Socio-Economic Research programme, an area of research introduced in RTD4, and in which two activity themes deal with the application of new technologies in education and the dissemination of innovative teaching. Second is the Telematics Applications programme, whose aim is to help develop a competitive supply of multimedia products and services including educational applications. Third is the Information Technologies programme, which is aimed more at generic solutions in areas such as multimedia systems, software technologies and high-performance computing and networking; its impact on educational telematics is therefore less direct than in the other two areas.

In LEONARDO (the EU's action programme for vocational training), distance and open learning are treated as a 'horizontal theme' – that is, they might be applied to any project within the framework of the programme. Distance and open learning are dealt with more explicitly in the EU's action programme for education, SOCRATES. Under the third chapter of SOCRATES, the Commission intends that the new technologies should help introduce the European dimension into open and distance learning. Specific priorities are to support transnational projects to:

- promote the use of new technologies in conventional ('face-to-face') education; and
- help develop pedagogical frameworks for integrating educational software into teaching.

The general objectives of the open and distance learning section of SOCRATES are:

- facilitating cooperation between users and producers;
- improving the skills of teachers, trainers and administrators in the use of the techniques;
- improving the quality and user-friendliness of products; and
- encouraging recognition of qualifications acquired through distance and open learning.

In Action 3.5 of the SOCRATES programme, the Commission offers support to adult education projects, with particular reference to those which promote the production of learning materials leading to a better understanding of the political, economic and administrative affairs of the EU. Particular emphasis is placed on the strengthening of cooperation in open and distance learning through the establishment of European partnerships and networks.

A number of other EU programmes also support educational telematics. Some are of particular interest to trainers and educators working with adults.

- The MEDIA programme was approved for the period 1996–2000 with the aim of helping stimulate the growth of the European audiovisual programme industry. One of its priorities is training for European professionals (e.g. virtual image designers, programme designers, new technology project leaders and so on), mainly in management and new audiovisual technologies.

- INFO 2000 was adopted in May 1996 to encourage firms to take advantage of developments in electronic publishing, including inter-active multimedia information services. INFO 2000 builds on an earlier programme, IMPACT, under which libraries, universities and small firms were encouraged to use telematics to provide electronic information services, including the development of interactive multimedia titles.

- Within the European Social Fund, the ADAPT initiative particularly focuses on information society projects, while the European Regional Development Fund has supported infrastructural investment in the new technologies in the least advantaged regions.

- Finally, the Commission's new programme for museums and art galleries (RAPHAEL) has supported pilot projects to make the cultural heritage more accessible through multimedia materials such as interactive CD (CD-i).

Examples of educational applications in the EU's programmes

Clearly the EU's interest and involvement is wide-ranging. It has an ambitious two-track policy goal, of attempting to turn Europe into both a learning society and an information society. An extraordinary number of its programmes are concerned in some way with supporting the development of educational telematics: in 1996, the Commission's Task Force on Educational Software and Multimedia identified at least nine programmes where the EU made a significant contribution to educational telematics (European Commission 1996). Just what does this mean in practice, how innovative is it, and how far does it touch upon the training and education of adults?

DELILAH

Designing and Evaluating Learning Innovations and Learning Applications

Aim: to investigate the actual and potential contribution of open
              and distance learning and advanced learning technologies
              in extending access to education and training for different
              groups, especially excluded ones

Programme: RTD4 (Targeted Socio-Economic Research)

What it's Synthesis of existing research on new ways of learning, compare about:
different national experieces of different organisational settings for learning and
accessibility of learning for less favoured groups, and develop approaches using
more effective mixes of new training products (especially multimedia products),
using an action-research, user-led environment, with partners in Germany,
Greece, Holland, Italy, Spain and Britain.

Co-ordinator: Tavistock Institute, London

UK partner: Manchester Metropolitan University

In SOCRATES, by contrast, the Commission has sponsored a large and diverse group
of projects. For example, in summer 1996 DG XXII approved 41 projects involving
288 partners from 18 nations, covering a wide range of projects from the development
of multimedia materials for teacher training to the compilation of databases of good
practice.

DG XXII has also selected a number of telematics-supported projects within the
LEONARDO programme. Examples include: a Devon-based consortium to provide
distance training for SMEs in the tourism sector in six countries via satellite
teleconferencing; a CD ROM database on vocational qualifications in the EU
(EURONETWORK), led by the National Council for Vocational Qualifications; and
a number of industry-specific language learning packages.

WORKBASE MULTIMEDIA EMPLOYEE TRAINING

Aim:	To improve employees' skills and develop a methodology to enable firms, trade unions and others to identify the training needs of individuals and organisations, using a multimedia toolkit
Funder:	European Commission through LEONARDO DA VINCI

What it's Development of a multimedia training needs analysis toolkit, about: focusing particularly on SMEs and emphasising literacy, numeracy and communications skills, across four member states.

Co-ordinator: Workbase Training (London)

Conclusion

In many ways, European policy towards telematics and learning is confused and therefore confusing. Although the Commission has tried to press for a coordinated approach to the use of telematics across its various education and training initiatives, it is hard enough to ensure common practice across the SOCRATES and LEONARDO programmes which are both managed by the same DG. There are probably twentyfive or so other programmes in which education and training play a significant role, and coordination across all of these is at best a long term process. Nevertheless, it is all but certain that Commission interest in this area will develop. Most adult educators will see this as a reasonable position for the Commission, given the exciting potential – as yet largely unrealised – of telematics to transform the education and training system. On top of this objective, the Commission is also highly aware that under the terms of the Maastricht Treaty, its powers in education and training are strictly limited to those activities which can best be carried out at the European level. Educational telematics – and multimedia in particular – looks to the Commission as though it is just such an activity. Although the EU will not overtake national agencies as a source of ideas and funding for the foreseeable future, it certainly makes sense to watch this space.

Further information

The European Commission is at: Rue de la loi 200, 1049 Brussels European Commission departments (known as Directorates General, or DGs) with a particularly important role in educational telematics are:

- DG V (Employment and Social Affairs) for the Structural Funds
- DG X (Audio-visual, Information and Culture) for the MEDIA programme
- DG XII (Science, Research and Development) for the RTD programmes
- DG XIII (Telecommunications, Information Society) for telematics applications, INFO 2000 and IMPACT – e-mail: telet@dg13.ce.be
- DG XXII (Education, Training) for SOCRATES and LEONARDO

EUROPA (European Commission home pages on the World Wide Web) is at: http.www.cec.lu
The Information Society Project Office (ISPO) can be contacted as follows:
Freephone on: 0800 962114
E-mail: ispo@ispo.cec.be
World Wide Web: http://www.ispo.cec.be/ispo

References

European Commission (1991) *Memorandum on Higher Education*, Office for Official Publications of the European Communities.

European Commission (1994), *Europe and the global information society*, Office for Official Publications of the European Communities.

European Commission (1995) *Teaching and Learning: towards the learning society*, Office for Official Publications of the European Communities.

European Commission (1996) *Educational Software and Multimedia: intermediate report*. Directorate-General XIII.

Riché-Magnier, M. and Metthey, J. (1995) 'Société de l'information: "New Deal" libéral ou nouvelle modèle de société?', *Revue du Marché commun et de l'Union européenne*, no. 390, pp. 417–22.

Sharp, M. (1993) 'The Community and new technologies', in J. Lodge (ed.) *The European Community and the Challenge of the Future*, Pinter.

Glossary

Audio conference: Voice-only connection for a meeting where one or more parties are not in the same physical location

Bulletin board: A form of conferencing through e-mail. An electronic pinboard:participants send mail to the electronic address of a communal bulletin board where it may be read by all parties who have access, and who may add messages

CAL: Computer Aided Learning

CBL: Computer Based Learning

CD-ROM: Compact Disk, Read-Only Memory:a plastic disk encoded with information accessed by integrated laser light and computer technologies

CMC: Computer Mediated Communication

Cybercafe: A coffee shop providing casual access to the Internet (as well as coffee); user pays for the time on-line

Digital information: Any information accessed via computer

DTP: Desk Top Publishing, using word-processing and graphics software to produce printed documents

E-mail: Electronic Mail:personal text-based communication via computer and phone line

FTP: File Transfer Protocol:allows transfer of files across a network

HTML: HyperText Markup Language – the language used to create Web documents

http: Hypertext transport protocol, indicating an address on the World Wide Web

Home Page: The main Web document for an organisation, group or individual

Hypertext: Collections of text, graphics, audio and/or video information that may be accessed one screen at a time, usually be clicking on highlighted words, in the order required by the user

Internet: Worldwide network of computer networks, with a common addressing system.

ISDN: Integrated Services Digital Network:an international standard for digital communications over telephone lines which allows the transmission of data (removing the need for a modem)

Interactive: User-controlled access to information, where the programme adjusts and responds to user input

JANET: Joint Academic NETwork; research and education network available in all UK universities, now upgraded to SUPER JANET

Mailbox: The location on the computer where an individual's e-mail is stored

Modem: MOdulator DEModulator – a device for converting computer data into, and from, a suitable form for transmission along telephone networks

Multimedia: The combination of different media, such as text, graphics, audio and video, to one resource

Net: Short for network eg, Internet

Network: Computer systems linked by communications channels

Newsgroup: Bulletin boards on the Internet covering a huge range of topics

Online: Currently connected to a network

Online service: Public computer service accessible via the telephone network; may offer storage and forwarding of e-mail, e-mail conferences and access to online databases. Fees are based on connection time

Real-time: When data input and output (almost) coincide; eg video-conferencing

Site: Source of on-screen information

Superhighway: Telecommunications channels and computer networks connected by telephone lines, cables and satellites

TBT: Technology Based Teaching

TLTP: Teaching and Learning Technology Projects -mainstream funding for UK Higher Education available in the early 1990s

Telecentre: A resource centre providing telematic services to a local community

Teleconferencing: The generic name for meetings where one or more parties involved are not in the same physical location. Communication may be by voice or video-link or with support from text or graphics

Telecottage: A telecentre in a rural location

Telematics: The convergence of computing and communication, integrating information and telecommunications technology

Telemedicine: Remote diagnosis, advice on surgical procedures or training using video conferencing

Telnet: A programme enabling a user to log-on to a remote computer over a network

Teleshopping: Shopping using videotex or an alternative online service

Teleworking: Any working practice where employees are based in a remote location from an employer, workers are mobile or a small company is remote from its major clients

URL: Uniform Resource Locator; the addressing system for the World Wide Web

Video conferencing: Live, two-way audio-visual computer-based communication

Videophone: Telephone with a screen and camera allowing a two-way video and audio link

Videotex: A system that transmits text and simple graphics over a public telephone network for access via an adapted television set:interaction takes place by using a keypad.

Voice mail: Voice messages digitised and stored for retrieval by the recipient

World Wide Web: Graphics-based tool for using the Internet

Notes on contributors

Martin Paul Buck is the Project Leader for the Building Learning Webs project at Camosun College, British Columbia, Canada and a Maths and English Adult Basic Education instructor. The project focuses on the development of electronic instructional modules to meet the learning needs of the Adult Basic Education community within and beyond the College. He is also responsible for training faculty and staff in telematics literacy. Contact: email: buck@camosun.bc.ca web site: http://abe.camosun.bc.ca

Sue Challis is the Project Development Officer for the Rural Broadnet Project at the University of Wolverhampton. The project is exploring the feasibility of using information technology to overcome barriers to education, training and other opportunities which may arise from rural isolation or tradition.
Contact: Telephone: 01902 323828; Fax: 01902 323960;
Email: BU1705@wbs.wlv.ac.uk

Peter Childs is a Senior Lecturer in Literary Studies and Academic Computing Co-ordinator in the School of Media, Critical, and Creative Arts at Liverpool John Moores University. His interests lie in how technology is going to change teaching methods and learning experiences over the next decade, having come to Higher Education after a career in computing. Recent projects have to an extent been an attempt to appraise the reactions of humanities lecturers and students to the presentation of text(s) in different electronic forms.
Contact: Telephone: 0151 231 5021

Dominic Dibble, a Teaching and Research Assistant, works in the Division of Educational Policy and Development at the University of Stirling co-ordinating the IT component on Environmental Education course. He has provided training and support for NewsWatcher, Usenet Newsreading package, Mosaic, and Netscape, and creating WWW pages. He is particularly interested in IT as means of facilitating group work.
Contact: Telephone 0141 563 1080
Email: d.dibble@stir.ac.uk

Jane Field, an Education and Development consultant, based in Northern Ireland, works with a number of universities across Europe and with community based groups in Northern Ireland and Ireland. Recent activities include managing a transnational project – Promoting Added Value through Evaluation – funded by the European Commission, under the Leonardo programme; and evaluating a Youthstart project in Dublin.
Contact: Telephone: 01960 368498; Fax: 01960 355005;
Email: janefield@c-fergus.demon.co.uk

John Field is Professor of Continuing Education at the University of Ulster. His research is on aspects of lifelong learning and human resource development in Northern Ireland and the European Union. He is editor of the *International Journal of University Adult Education*.
Contact: Email: jl.field@ulst.ac.uk

Brian Gilding is the Chairman for International Programmes at the University of Bradford Management Centre.
Contact: through Rob McClements (see below)

Maude Gould divides her time between the Open Learning Centre of an FE college and teaching at the University of Greenwich on the in-service Cert Ed (FE) and BA Education and Training progammes. She previously taught in FE for many years before becoming Staff Development Co-ordinator at an inner London college.
Contact: Telephone: 0171 320 3054 Fax: 0171 320 3027
Email: m.gould@gre.ac.uk

Paul Helm is a Distance Learning Adviser in the Department of Continuing Education at the University of Bradford. He has taught adults in Liverpool, South Wales and Bradford on a variety of courses, from Access courses to English Literature to Information Technology. His main interests are telematics-based learning, electronic communities and technology in business and management training.
Contact: Telephone: 01274 383338; Fax: 01274 383218
Email: P.Helm@bradford.ac.uk

Andy Leal, from the Plymouth College of Further Education, has responsibility for introducing flexibility into the college and wider community; advising senior staff on Further and Higher Education Funding Council funding; and developing and submitting bids.
Contact : Telephone: 01752 385870; Fax: 01752 385831

Tony Lewis is currently Programme Director for the University of Greenwich BA (Hons) Education and Training. He previously taught in FE colleges, before working in educational television and eventually moving into teacher training for the post-16 sector.
Contact: Telephone: 0171 320 3054; Fax: 0171 320 3027;
Email: d.a.lewis@gre.ac.uk

Jill Mannion Brunt is a Senior Research Fellow at the University of Sheffield, working in the Trent Institute for Health Services Research, in the Faculty of Medicine. Her responsibilities lie in Research Training for Health Service workers. Her background is in Adult Education, and her previous post was Assistant Principal at the Northern College in Barnsley, with responsibility for Student Support Services. She has worked in the field of workplace learning and employee development.
Contact: Telephone: 0114 2768555; Fax: 0114 2724095;
Email: j.m.brunt@sheffield.ac.uk

Rob McClements from the University of Bradford Management Centre is the Director of the European Telematics Group. The Group uses a range of technologies and techniques to develop multi-media tools for teaching and learning.
Contact: Telephone: 01274 384440; Fax: 01274 384444;
Email: j.r.mcclements@bradford.ac.uk

Aideen McGinley is the Chief Executive Officer of Fermanagh District Council, with responsibility for Regional Community and Economic Development. She has extensive experience in community and economic development.
Contact: Telephone: 01365 325050; Fax: 01365 322024

Stephen McNair is Associate Director for Research and Development at the National Institute of Adult Continuing Education (NIACE), with special responsibility for Higher Education and for Telematics. He is also a Higher Education Adviser to the

Department for Education and Employment (DfEE), working on a range of issues to do with HE and its relevance to the world of work.
Contact: Telephone: 0116 204 4200; Fax: 0116 285 4514

Lisa McRory is a Research Assistant at Liverpool John Moores University, where her current work involves Content Researcher and Co-ordinator for the Text, Theory, Event CD-ROM project; on-going evaluation of the On-Demand Publishing project; and provision of specialist humanities computing support to staff via the MCCA Multimedia Courseware Development Group (MCDG). She is particularly interested in user response, not just to the projects under the remit of the MCDG, but to IT provision, support and the use of educational software in teaching and learning generally.
Contact: Telephone: 01273 69611
Email: l.m.mcrory@livjm.ac.uk

Kate O'Dubhchair is a Senior Lecturer in the Faculty of Informatics at the University of Ulster. Her responsibilities include Continuing Education and Rural Telematics Outreach. She has extensive experience in applied telematics and the humanisation of technology.
Contact: Telephone: 01504 375370; Fax: 01504 375470;
Email: KM.ODubhchair@ulst.ac.uk

Sarah Porter is a Research Assistant at Liverpool John Moores University, with responsibility for the co-ordination of the On-Demand Publishing Project. This involves the design and development of WWW-compatible on-line materials using HTML; the development and maintenance of the project WWW site and user instruction and education. She is interested in issues relating to the user-centred design of electronic materials and the use of IT in teaching and learning centres upon the potential of the Internet and the World Wide Web to offer increased and enhanced access to electronic learning materials.
Contact: Telephone: 0151 231 5056;
Email: S.C.Porter@livjm.ac.uk

Geoff Rhen, a lecturer at Murdoch University in Western Australia, has held the posts of State President and national Secretary for the Australian Society for educational Technology. His activities include the first use in Western Australia of satellite video conferencing, audiographics to remote communities and the application of the Internet to educational delivery.
Contact: Telephone: 00 61 9360 2844; Fax: 00 61 9310 4929

Alan Robinson is a senior lecturer in Adult and Continuing Education at the University of Ulster. He has been working in university and continuing education from 1973. His interest in educational interactive technologies dates from 1984.
Contact: Telephone: 01265 324628; Fax: 01265 40918

Malcolm Ryan is currently on part-time secondment from his full-time lecturing post at the University of Greenwich, to the university's Academic Development Group where he is helping to raise the awareness of colleagues to the potential of new technology in supporting teaching and learning. His background is in drama, the media and resource-based learning. He previously taught in schools and worked as a media

resources officer within the ILEA before entering teacher education.
Contact: Telephone: 0171 320 3054; Fax: 0171 320 3027;
Email: m.ryan@gre.ac.uk

Kate Sankey is a Lecturer of Environmental Education in the Division of Educational Policy and Development at the University of Stirling. Her interest developed in modern communication technologies from the realisation of the potential available for access to information and opportunities for enhancing the collaborative learning experience for students; relevant to her work with the part time undergraduate degree programme and the development of short courses for adult and continuing education.
Contact: Telephone: 01786 467944; Fax: 01786 463398;
Email: c.e.sankey@stir.ac.uk

John Smith is the Videoconferencing Project Manager at City College, Norwich. He also has some responsibility for the development of Teaching and Learning with Technology in the college.
Contact: Telephone: 01603 773281; Fax: 01603 773013;
Email: jsmith@ccn.ac.uk

Adrian Vranch, from the University of Plymouth, is the Academic Developments Manager, Computing Service. He is responsible for research and development initiatives in the Computing Service, especially in developing collaborative projects with lecturers and other staff in the university and with staff in other institutions. Research interests and publications include distance learning, telematics, multimedia and electronic communication, with a focus on development of techniques to measure the effectiveness of these technologies and their practical impact on human interaction.
Contact: Telephone: 01626 325834; Fax: 01626 325837;
Email: avranch@plymouth.ac.uk

Betty Walsh is a lecturer in Distance Education at Murdoch University, Western Australia. She has published and presented a number of papers on issues connected with educational technology; coordinated a project encouraging academics to use Internet services and developed course materials available through the Internet and World Wide Web for a veterinary science unit. She is responsible for videoconferencing at Murdoch University.
Contact: Telephone: 00 16 9360 2844;
Email:- e-walsh@cleo.murdoch.edu.au

Ray Winders, as Telematics Developments Co-ordinator at the University of Plymouth, is responsible for promotion and effective delivery using the full range of satellite and terrestrial technologies. He is the Director of several funded projects in live transmission by satellite, audio-conferencing and data delivery.
Contact: Telephone: 01752 233927; Fax: 01752 233159;
Email: rwinders@plym.ac.uk

Also published by NIACE:

Learners on the superhighway? Access to learning via electronic communications
Keith Yeomans
ISBN 1 872941 96 6
1996, 112pp, £6.50

A report of a study tour visiting policy-makers and practitioners in electronic communications and education in the United States and Canada. The greatest observed difference between Britain and North America is not the availability or use of technology. Rather, it is the level of informed awareness by policy-makers and practitioners of the issues, needs and resources relating to equitable access, particularly for disadvantaged groups.

Yeomans concludes that the information superhighway as presenting both opportunities and threats to access, and sets out an agenda for promoting equitable access in Britain.

' . . . a great deal of useful information . . . education and training providers would be advised to read it' (*The Lecturer*)

Adults count too: Mathematics for empowerment
Roseanne Benn
ISBN 1 86201 007 2
Publication date: June 1997, approx 176pp, £14.95

More and more adults are learning mathematics, either for work-related purposes, or as a qualification leading to a desired course of study. *Adults count too* examines the low level of numeracy in our society, the reasons why this is critical and the forces acting on adults which contribute to this state of affairs. Written to encourage the development of a curriculum which is tailored to the priorities and lives of individuals, Benn argues that mathematics is not a value-free construct, but is imbued with elitist notions which exclude and mystify. The book seeks alternative approaches to teaching mathematics which recognise the sophisticated mathematical techniques and ideas used in everyday work, domestic and leisure.

This book will be of interest to adult educators who teach mathematics or to mathematics educators who teach adults.

Imagining tomorrow: adult education for transformation
Marjory Mayo
ISBN 1 86201 006 4
Publication date: June 1997, approx 176pp, £14.95

A study of the increasing importance of community and workplace adult education in the First and Third worlds. Mayo looks at the impact of globalisation, economic restructuring and the enhanced role of community and voluntary organisations in the provision of education. She presents the case for wider understanding of the context and possibilities for local development as part of longer-term strategies for transformation.

Mayo looks at the implications of adult learning for sustainable development for social justice, defined by local communities themselves. She takes case studies from Tanzania, Cuba, India and Nicaragua as well as from the industrialised 'North' to illustrate her themes. The book concludes by focussing on issues of culture, identity, diversity and changing consciousness; and the role of community education in strengthening collective confidence to effect social transformation.

Words in edgeways: radical learning for social change
Jane Thompson
Publication date: June 1997, approx 176pp, £14.95

Jane Thompson's books and essays have inspired and validated the work of radical practitioners in adult and community education not only in Britain, but also overseas – particularly in Ireland, Australia, New Zealand, Canada and the United States.

This is a collection of extracts, essays and conference presentations, written over a 20-year period, on working class and women's education. This volume covers the application of Marxist, sociological and feminist analysis to adult education; connections between the women's movement and adult education, and a collection of writings by women learners whose lives were restricted by poverty and family violence.

This book will be useful to students on adult and continuing education courses at Diploma and Masters level. It will also be of relevance to staff development activity, conferences and workshops in which matters of curriculum, political education, participatory learning, citizenship and social change are being discussed. Practitioners in adult learning and community education who are concerned about disadvantage and issues of inclusion and exclusion will also find the book valuable.

Ethics and education for adults in a late modern society
Peter Jarvis
ISBN 1 86201 014 5 (hbk)
ISBN 1 86201 015 3 (pbk)
Publication date: June 1997, approx 256pp, £35.00 (hbk), £17.95 (pbk)

This new book by Peter Jarvis analyses recent developments in the education of adults from an ethical perspective. Based upon the argument that there is only one universal good, and that all other moral goods are cultural and relative, he develops the position that education for adults is a site within which human morality is worked out. Examining both traditional topics, such as teaching and learning, and more recent ones, such as the education market, distance education and the learning society, Jarvis argues that educators need to be critically aware of the ethical implications of these developments. This is a topical book which should be of interest to everybody involved in education at every level and every age group.

Peter Jarvis is currently Professor of Continuing Education at the University of Surrey and Adjunct Professor of Adult Education at the University of Georgia, USA. He was previously Head of Department of Educational Studies at the University of Surrey. He is the author and editor of more than twenty books. He is also the editor of *The International Journal of Lifelong Education.*

Adults learning
ISSN 0955 2308

Subscription rates: £30 (institutions); extra copies @ £15 each
£17.50 (individuals)
£15 (concessions for part-time tutors and adult learners)

The need for a professional journal for those concerned with adult learning has never been greater than now. The majority of students in further and higher education in Britain are adults. More and more awareness of the importance of adults as learners is being shown by government, the media, employers and trade unions. In a quickly-changing environment it is vital to keep abreast of current issues and initiatives, debates and events.

Adults learning is the only UK-wide journal solely devoted to matters concerning adult learning. It carries the latest news on policy and practice, and is published ten times a year by NIACE. It is a forum for adult educators and trainers to exchange information, share practice, network and engage in dialogue with fellow professionals.

In-depth features, commentaries, reviews and case studies, together with news of courses, conferences and resources, make *Adults learning* essential reading for policy-makers and practitioners, tutors (both full-time and part-time) in universities and further education colleges, staff in voluntary organisations who are developing learning opportunities, and trainers in industry seeking advice on skills development.

Studies in the education of adults
ISSN 0266 0830

Subscription rates: UK £20 individual;   £30 institutional
Overseas surface mail: £22/US$40 individual;   £33/US$59 institutional
Overseas airmail: £25/US$45 individual;   £38/US$67 institutional

An international refereed journal published twice a year (April and October) by NIACE. It is addressed to academic specialists, postgraduate students, practitioners and educational managers who wish to keep abreast of scholarship, theory-building and empirical research in the broad field of education and training for adults.

Studies in the education of adults publishes theroetical, empirical and historical studies from all sectors of post-initial education and training, and aims to provide a forum for debate and development of key concepts in education and training. With feature articles and book reviews, the journal provides indispensable analysis of current developments and thinking.

A full publications catalogue is available from NIACE at 21 De Montfort Street, Leicester, LE1 7GE, England. Alternatively visit our Web site on the Internet:

www.niace.org.uk